Godly Grandparenting

A Christian Guide for Today's Families

Godly Grandparenting: A Christian Guide for Today's Families

Ben E. Dickerson, Ph.D.
Derrel R. Watkins, Ph.D.

ISBN-13: 9780979017483
ISBN-10: 0979017483

Library of Congress Control Number: 2007928535

Copyright © 2008 by Power Publishing
All rights reserved.

Unless otherwise indicated, all scripture is taken from the HOLY BIBLE, NEW INTERNATIONAL VERSION®. Copyright © 1973, 1978, 1984 International Bible Society. Used by permission of Zondervan. All rights reserved.

All rights reserved. No part of this book may be reproduced without written permission from the publisher, except by a reviewer who may quote brief passages in a review; nor may any part of this book be reproduced, stored in a retrieval system or transmitted in any form or other without written permission from the publisher.

This book is manufactured in the United States of America.

Power Publishing
5641 W. 73rd St.
Indianapolis, IN 46278
(317) 347-1051
www.powerpublishinginc.com

Cover Design: Parada Design

Godly Grandparenting

A Christian Guide for Today's Families

Ben E. Dickerson, Ph.D.

Derrel R. Watkins, Ph. D.

Power Publishing Incorporated
Indianapolis, IN

Ben's Dedication

To my dad, Robert Ben Dickerson.
Had he lived, he would have been the best grandfather ever!
To my mother, Lois Dickerson.
Her grandchildren knew how wonderful this grandmother's love could be. She always went the second mile for them.

To all 16 of my grandchildren who make life an adventure and blessing for me daily. Brent, Brian, Derek, Haley, Jack, Jake, Luke, Aaron, Jordan, Gabrielle, Harley, Mackenzie, Moriah, Ari, Michael, Rachael, and also my two great-grandchildren, Caden and Bradyn. I love you all.

To all the Foster Grandparents I've had the privilege to know. You taught me, "To live is to love and to love is to live."

Derrel's Dedication

I want to dedicate this book to Janis, the woman who I believe embodies more of the best qualities of grandmothering than any person I have ever known. She is mother of my two wonderful children, Derrelynn and Stephen, and the grandmother of our grandsons, Jason and Vincent, and our "bonus granddaughters," Sarah and Emily.

I would also like to pay tribute to my wonderful daughter-in-law, Carma, and my fine son-in-law, Leigh. I consider them to be as much a part of my family as my biological children. Without them I would not have the joy of being a grandfather.

Know the Authors and Contributors

Ben Dickerson and Derrel Watkins have known each other for four decades. Ben and Derrel first met while representing two different educational institutions. They discovered they had a number of common interests. Both were people persons, both desired to make a difference with their lives, and both based their work on their Christian faith.

Ben has had the opportunity and benefited greatly from his involvement with youth groups such as Boy Scouts, FFA, and Christian camps. Additionally, he had what he calls a privilege to be a faculty member at several well-known universities throughout the country. Furthermore, his experience in the military provided exposure to some of the best leaders this country has, which taught him how to lead. Ben's undying interest has been dogs and their well-being. He is blessed by having a blended family that has provided him with many opportunities to expand his grandparenting career. Ben is known for his involvement with his students beyond the classroom. They felt welcome in his home and joined him in coauthoring articles for magazines and making presentations at national and regional meetings.

Derrel Watkins is a man with a multitude of interests from coffee beans to theology, psychology, ministry, and an incredible desire to learn more of just about everything. He has made significant contributions to higher education whether in colleges, universities, or seminaries. He is most known for his love for students and his willingness to help them in any way possible. Derrel, a Christian, relies heavily on his faith, especially the scriptures, to know how best to apply his life where it counts the most for his Lord and Savior. Derrel has been blessed with two wonderful children—a daughter and a son. His daughter made a granddaddy out of him in 1984 with the birth of his number one grandson, Jason. His son added another grandson, Vincent, nine years later. In addition, his blessings include a favorite daughter-in-law (she is the only one) and a great son-in-law who contributed two "bonus granddaughters," Sarah and Emily, to the family. Derrel loves most types of music and sings almost anything from classical to country western to hymns.

Both men feel a strong calling to utilize their God-given gifts to encourage others to maximize themselves for as long as possible. Likewise both men continue to be students of the scriptures, the family, and the life course as it continues to change through time. Ben and Derrel are avid readers. When they are at national meetings they utilize any spare time to visit the closest book displays to see what is new. Both these individuals make every effort to maintain a lifelong commitment to their students. Their desire is that their students will move beyond where they have been and create new pathways to the discovery of knowledge.

Ben and Derrel have been extremely fortunate in meeting some very talented people throughout their professional careers. Among that number are three that were asked to write chapters for this book. Kay Smith, lawyer turned social worker, is the author of Chapter 9, *Grandparenting and the Law*. Kay reflects so much in her life what we would like to see in our own. She is a servant of the people, devoted to helping them in whatever way possible. She often mentions how important her husband has been by encouraging her to make the transition from a prosperous career as an attorney to one that is seldom known for the income it generates. Ben first met Kay while she was a student in the Oklahoma Leadership Academy on Aging. It was easy to recognize quickly that Kay was both unique in her desire to serve and also a very bright woman able to grasp problems and solve them quickly. She quickly responded to our request to write a chapter for this book, knowing that it could be used to help many.

Lance Robertson the author of Chapter 5, *Grandparents Raising Grandchildren*, is one of the best known individuals in the aging network throughout the state of Oklahoma. He has served at a university as codirector of a center for the study of aging, selected as executive director of a regional professional association, and known for his consulting and speaking gifts. Lance, reared by his grandparents, exemplifies how grandparents can make a difference in a grandchild's life. He gives his grandparents considerable credit for the man he has become.

Jim Hughes, author of Chapter 12, *Long Distance Grandparenting*, exemplifies what a strong faith can mean in a life filled with a number of unexpected challenges. His first wife died at an early age, leaving him the responsibility to raise three children. At the same time he had set a goal to pursue a college degree with a hope of advancing into graduate school. He often mentions how, during these times, God met all his needs and made the way for him to become what he believed God had called him to do. Jim not only finished a college degree but also complete a Ph.D. in Gerontology at the University of Nebraska. Since graduation, he has been an adjunct faculty member and a student minister, as well as authored numerous articles, notebooks, and other valuable publications. He also has served as a minister in several churches, helping him to gain a greater understanding of human behavior in difficult times. Jim has remarried and continues to devote himself to his family and his calling. One of his biggest challenges in the past few years has been how to be the grandfather he wants to be when his grandchildren live so far away. If anyone can meet this challenge with success it is Jim Hughes.

Acknowledgements

Writing any kind of book requires a team effort. Many individuals helped us fulfill our long-held desire to share these thoughts and experiences about grandparenting with interested people throughout the world.

To begin, a big "thank you" is given to Tad Long and Janet Schwind of Power Publishing for their vision and encouragement. Their knowledge of the publishing world is reflected in the professionalism of their work. Janet's tireless editing of the manuscript has gone beyond anything we could have anticipated.

One of the most important aspects of writing this book has been the privilege of working daily with Dr. Derrel Watkins. As my friend and mentor, he constantly amazed me with the vast array of knowledge he shared with me as his partner in this one-of-a-kind adventure. Derrel's Christian faith has always shown brightly for me and everyone else involved with this project. I count my time with Derrel and his wife, Janis, as one of the most rewarding experiences in my life.

My wife, Florence, has been the unsung hero in this endeavor. She has been our human library, our sounding board, and an unbelievable help in more ways than could be counted to make this book a reality. For her unconditional acceptance of Derrel and I writing and disrupting the order at home, I thank her.

Kay Smith, Lance Robertson and Dr. Jim Hughes, the three individuals we asked to help us in completing this book, have been willing to go beyond the call of duty. It is difficult to find the words needed to express our heart-felt thanks for the significant contribution each of them made.

Ken Arthur, my longtime friend, was always available to join with us to discover the right word or phrase needed to improve our communication with the reader. Ken continues to amaze me with his gifts of intellect, servanthood and creativity. He is an awesome human being with a heart bigger than life itself.

This acknowledgement would be incomplete if I did not name my beloved Texas A&M University, its faculty, staff and students. They gave me the confidence and determination to "Be all I can be with the gifts God has given me." What a privilege to be called a "Fighting Texas Aggie."

Finally, I would be remiss if I did not recognize the numerous grandparents and grandchildren who shared their stories and suggestions about the most important emerging career in our lifetime, grandparenting.

Above all I thank my God for his everlasting love and grace to me. It is my desire more than anything to honor and serve him by making a difference in the lives of people around the world.

Ben E. Dickerson
June 2008

One of the great delights of my life has been the times over the years that I have had the honor of working with Ben E. Dickerson. His commitment to his family and his students has been exemplary. During the weeks we worked together on this book, I came to know him better and I continue to appreciate this man of extraordinary character and Christian commitment. He has an amazing ability to conceptualize the needs of persons of every generation. He not only understands the needs of grandparents, but he is concerned about the special needs of people in their everyday-lived life. I am truly blessed to have the privilege of working with such a friend.

I want to also acknowledge the training I received at Ouachita Baptist University, Southwestern Seminary, the University of Georgia, and the University of Texas at Arlington. Three professors stand out because of what they meant to me at crucial times in my life. One was my major professor at Ouachita, Professor of Sociology, Dr. Randolph Quick. Dr. James Williams was my mentor and colleague who introduced me to Gerontology. The other was my mentor and professional guide, Dr. David L. Levine at the University of Georgia, who encouraged me to embrace and evaluate knowledge from many sources and apply that knowledge to helping people.

Throughout my life course, God has placed very special people in my path to provide exceptional support and guidance. Only God can provide them with the recognition they deserve.

Above all, my wife, Dr. Janis Nutt Watkins, who has stuck by my side through thick and thin for over 47 years as my best critic and most ardent supporter, has made this effort possible. She, in my opinion, is the ideal model of a modern godly grandparent. It is my prayer that this book will be beneficial and a blessing to grandparents and potential grandparents as the years go by.

Derrel R. Watkins
June 2008

Preface

This book on grandparenting was not conceived with the purpose of having another publication to our credit. After more than three decades of studying and practicing the science and art of aging, we discovered the value of an often overlooked member of today's multigenerational family.

As we observed and interacted with grandparents of all ages for over thirty years, we agreed that a readable and practical book about grandparenting was needed. In our research we discovered a number of books, periodicals, and journal articles written on the subject. A few emphasized the importance of spirituality in fulfilling this role. Our intention is to complement those publications, recognizing the value of a solid faith foundation that maximizes the positive effects grandparents can have on their grandchildren.

Hopefully our book has integrated what we have learned from the behavioral sciences, theology, our own experiences as grandparents and listening to the personal experiences of other grandparents and grandchildren. Such a synthesis will provide a value-added property to this publication.

As a reader please keep in mind that our motivation to write this book is our belief that anyone from the perspective of any faith persuasion can become a godly grandparent. We pray that what we say will go beyond the words in this book and give the readers, regardless of what position they hold in their family, the center stage. We hope that you will recognize the importance of wisdom in making application of the suggestions offered in these pages. We hope that they will be as much a blessing to you as studying this material has been to us.

We encourage you to look at the expanding definition of grandparenting as a career. No matter which type of grandparenting you identify with, read the chapters identifying and describing the types mentioned.

As you grasp a better understanding of grandparenting, we encourage you to reflect on the important contribution made by our ethnic grandparents. There is much to be learned from the rich heritage of every ethnic group.

Finally, pay attention to the laws affecting grandparenting. Many public policies have ignored the needs of grandparents and we encourage you to let your government representatives know of your concerns as well.

Greater clarity was made possible by the utilization of various translations of the Bible. The New International Version (NIV) is our basic translation. However we did make use of the New Living Translation (NLT), the Phillips Translation, and the King James Version (KJV). We appreciate the availability of versions of Holy Scripture in a language that can be clearly understood by everyone. Once you complete the reading of this book we recommend that you read it a second time and share it with other grandparents, adult children, and grandchildren as well. Some may want to have a social gathering where questions are raised and answers are sought. We did not have space in this book to cover every possible situation. We hope you will make this the beginning of a process that will enable you to grow even as grandparenting is growing in importance in our society and around the world.

Contents

Dedications *4*
Know the Authors and Contributors *6*
Acknowledgements *9*
Preface *12*

Chapter 1	Contemporary Grandparenting *17*
Chapter 2	Single Grandparenting *33*
Chapter 3	Great-Grandparenting *53*
Chapter 4	Grandparenting in Blended Families *71*
Chapter 5	Grandparents Raising Grandchildren *85*
Chapter 6	Ethnicity as a Resource in Grandparenting *105*
Chapter 7	Grandparents Achieving Spiritual Well-Being *125*
Chapter 8	Grandparents and Their Adult Children *139*
Chapter 9	Grandparenting and the Law *155*
Chapter 10	Grandparents and Their College Age Grandchildren *171*
Chapter 11	Surrogate Grandparenting *185*
Chapter 12	Long Distance Grandparenting *197*
Chapter 13	Grandparenting Today and Tomorrow *213*

chapter 1

CONTEMPORARY GRANDPARENTING

> DO NOT BE AFRAID OR DISCOURAGED, FOR THE LORD IS THE ONE WHO GOES BEFORE YOU. HE WILL BE WITH YOU; HE WILL NEITHER FAIL YOU NOR FORSAKE YOU.
> DEUTERONOMY 31:8 NLT

> TO EXIST IS TO CHANGE; TO CHANGE IS TO MATURE; TO MATURE IS TO GO ON CREATING ONESELF ENDLESSLY.
> HENRI BERGSON

Ruth, a sophomore in college, stopped by her grandmother's house on the way to her parents' home for spring break. Her grandmother listened eagerly to her granddaughter's chatter about college life and the courses she was taking. Ruth said, "Grandma, you probably don't know all this new computer language we students have to learn. In my computer class we are discussing kilobytes, megabytes, gigabytes, terabytes and things like that. In fact, I have to spend a lot of time during my spring break writing a 12 page term paper." Her grandmother asked, "Well...are you going to 'Google' the research for your term paper? In my computer class at the Shepherd Center at First Church the young teacher said that would save a lot of time.[1]"

This story illustrates one of the major ways grandparenting has changed in a computer driven society. When grandparenting is the topic of conversation nowadays we are hearing a new set of jargon such as *fly-in grandparent*, *bonus grandparent*, *grandparenting power*, *wisdom giver*, and *serial grandparents*. Likewise when computers take center stage in conversations, we're hearing a whole new language. Today we hear words like *kilobyte, megabyte, gigabyte*, and soon we will be hearing of *terabyte*, and *petabyte*. Everything in our lives is now somehow influenced by computers, the Internet, high definition television, wireless telephones, cell-phones, digital cameras, webphones, etc.

What does all of this advanced technology mean to family relationships when grandparents spend so much time trying to learn so many new skills? To begin answering such a question, let's take a closer look at where computers and other devices are influencing most of our relationships. It is, in fact, difficult these days to separate technology from relationships. For example, in the past we may have used pencil and paper to write a letter, put a three cent stamp on the envelope, and put it in the mail. We expected the letter to get to our family or friend within a week. When we received a telephone call we usually had to rush to the room where the telephone was attached to the wall. The family had only one telephone and it was on a table in the living room and could not be moved to

---

[1] This story is used for illustration only. It, like most of the stories in this book, unless otherwise indicated, is a composite drawn from stories told the authors in conferences with grandparents.

other parts of the house. Today, seldom do we reach for pen and paper or a telephone that is connected to the wall to send messages to one another. Instead, we reach for the laptop or the keyboard and begin speaking to someone at any time, any place through e-mail. Or, we reach in our pocket or purse to send or receive a telephone call or text message on our cell phone. Technology, it seems, has caught up with what was science fiction when we were growing up. Most can remember the comic strip where Dick Tracy could call his staff on a wrist video watch. Today, grandparents, via a video webcam mounted on the computer monitor, can not only speak to their grandchildren but instantly observe their growth spurts. This technology, regardless of its shortcomings, has spread throughout almost every area of our lives, such as dating, family, education, entertainment, travel, and religion.

It's easy to see how technology has blended with grandparenting. In fact, this blending has been so successful that we are now faced with some new realities of grandparenting.

New Realities of Grandparenting

Traditionally, grandparents were respected in the home and in the community. They owned the land and their knowledge was appreciated. Family life was essentially what some refer to as "country living." Families, including grandparents, children, and grandchildren, lived in one house, ate in the same kitchen, and everyone had specific chores that helped keep the farm producing and providing enough money for the family to survive. In this setting grandparents were seen as a source of "how to" knowledge. They were solid rocks on which the family built a strong value system.

Grandparents in Bible times demonstrated what it meant to follow biblical teachings in every aspect of life. They relied heavily on God's guidance and believed in keeping the Ten Commandments. Those who were faithful saw the fruits of their lives lived out in their grandchildren. One example of this is seen in 2 Timothy 3:16-17, where the apostle Paul reminds the young man, Timothy, of the importance of his grandmother Lois. She, along with his mother Eunice, was responsible for shaping Timothy's character.

Although the number of years grandparents had with their grandchildren was short in previous generations, they equipped the family with what it needed to survive and prosper. Now, as we are moving into what some call the "postmodern era," we often wonder how we have strayed from reliance on God's Word as our guide to a "Disneyworld" of multiple choices and styles. We now live in a world where what people believe about right and wrong is flexible and almost ignores biblical teachings. The trend among younger generations is to reject absolute standards. Sources of values such as the Bible, church doctrine, and the rule of law are no longer accepted as ultimate authority.

As the old Alka-Seltzer slogan stated, "Perhaps the circumstances won't change; but you can." If grandparents are to maintain a positive presence in their grandchildren's lives, they must try to understand the needs of their grandchildren and make changes in their own thinking where possible. It is not necessary for grandparents to throw away their values in order to fit in. It is important, however, that they try to understand what their children and grandchildren are facing in the everyday world. To gain such understanding, new realities must be identified and explored:

Longer life. In 1935, when the Social Security Act was passed, a child born that year was expected to live only 57 years. After World War II, changes in lifestyles and medical treatment have increased the likelihood that grandchildren will have their grandparents at least an additional 20 years. Baby Boomer grandparents (those born immediately after World War II) may well expect to dynamically expand the number of years of grandparent-grandchildren relationships. Think of the wisdom and life experiences these grandparents can share with the babies of their children. Family stories, legacies, and anecdotes which in previous generations might have been lost can now be passed on. Grandparents provide "history" and continuity. For example, most children rebel when their parents talk of "the good old days." However, the same phrase coming from a grandparent carries more weight. After all, to a child, grandparents really are "old" and their past has more meaning. A child saw Tom Brokaw on television and turned and looked at this grandfather. He asked, "Gramps, did you fight in the Second World War?"

The grandfather answered, "Yes, see the pictures on the wall?"

"Gramps, tell me about it. What did you do? Were you a hero?"

This gave the grandfather an opportunity to explain that anyone can be a hero. He explained the meaning of the values that caused the soldiers to fight that war and what those values continue to mean in his life today.

New family types. The most familiar type of family is made up of husband-wife-children, with grandparents living nearby. However, this is no longer the norm in most communities. Following World War II a variety of family types have become more prominent, including single parent families; blended families as a result of divorce, death and remarriage; marriage of single parents with children; never married families; and homosexual couples raising children. How many of these family types do you know of in your community? You may be surprised that most if not all these types are your neighbors. When you think of the stories in the Bible, how many family types can you name? As you read through this book, biblical family types are identified and biblical principles are used as the model for godly grandparenting.

Frequent family moves. Most families do not live their whole lives in one location. In many rural areas and small towns, there are not enough jobs available for children who grow up there. The average worker today changes jobs up to five times during his or her working years. Often this means moving the family from one part of the country to another and sometimes to another country in even another part of the world. This is especially true of a person who earns a college degree or receives specialized technical training.

Only a small percentage return to their home towns or to work in the family business. This reality is drawing attention to the importance of appreciating and strengthening family relationships. Technology is making it possible to maintain close contact, but distance is making it harder to have physical contact. Physical presence, however, is important to close family relationships and cannot be fully experienced with technological devices. Many grandparents are moving to new communities, near their children and grandchildren, in an attempt to maintain this close personal relationship.

Education throughout life. In the early years of the 20th century, earning a high school diploma was a goal achieved by only a few. Since the middle of the 20th century high school diplomas have become more common. Today, college graduation or receiving a technical training certificate is the important "rite of passage" that at one time belonged to high school graduation. Older people are completing their high school education and pursuing college degrees in ever increasing numbers. Community colleges are offering more continuing education and adult education classes especially designed for people in their later years. Men and women in their middle and later years are attending specialized classes at these colleges to learn such things as carpentry, woodworking, art, music, computer usage, small engine repair, refrigeration, plumbing, etc. Some are earning graduate degrees and entering professions formerly populated by younger people. Almost every college in America can identify an increasing number of grandmothers and grandfathers among their students. Most major universities are making online courses and degrees available so that people do not necessarily have to leave home to get a college education. A significant number of grandparents are taking advantage of these new offerings.

"Farming out" family responsibilities. Traditionally, grandparents often served as the daycare providers for preschool children in the family. Then programs such as kindergarten and daycare centers took children out of their homes earlier. When the economy changed, it became necessary for both parents to work outside the home. In many cases families did not live near grandparents. Daycare and preschool programs became a necessity. Values education and survival skills became the business of schools, churches, synagogues and the media (via television and the Internet) instead of families.

Multiple jobs during the family history. Although the general population of Americans seems to have believed families with one wage earner was the ideal, in reality multiple wage earners were necessary to pay for the things most families felt they needed. It was common for both father and mother to be employed full time, and teenage children to be gainfully employed part-time. Today, in a growing number of extended families, grandparents and even great-grandparents are employed as well. This situation limits the amount of time the family has together. A common problem can be seen in families where there are scheduling conflicts. For example, the husband works the evening shift and the wife works a day shift. Even on weekends family members may be pulled in different directions so that there is virtually no time for a shared meal or a time to sit together and talk.

Lawsuits. At the beginning of the 21st century, a teenager in Florida filed suit in family court to divorce his parents. This had never been done before in America. Often, when there is a death, divorce or remarriage, there are provisions involving children whereby grandparents are either neglected in the settlement or restricted from active involvement with their grandchildren. Sometimes in cases of abuse, chemical dependency, or neglect, grandparents file suit against adult children to take custody of and assume guardianship of their grandchildren (in some states the legal term is conservator). In another example, two adult children go to court to have a parent who needs 24/7 care placed in a nursing home. At the same time the grandchildren feel that the parents were being unfair and that grandmother could come live with them and that they would share in the responsibility of caring for her. The grandchildren filed suit in court to get a restraining order to keep their parents from having grandmother placed in a nursing home.

More housing choices. In the past, people preferred to "age in place"—in other words, in their own homes. Nowadays, many older people choose to downsize their homes or move into group living centers where they experience what Faith Popcorn[2] calls "cocooning." Older folks enjoy the communities' advantages of guarded gates to protect them from the common dangers they used to face in their old neighborhoods. It was also commonly expected that older people would move in with one of their adult children. Some convert their garages into apartments for their older, semi-dependent parents. Others build a small house on the property near their homes where the older parent will have some privacy, but live nearby in case of an emergency. Many more affluent older people are moving into specially designed retirement communities. Sometimes, but not always, these communities are only a short driving distance from their children and grandchildren.

Better communication. Initially the mail service (now called "snail mail") was the way grandparents maintained contact with their adult children and grandchildren wherever they lived. Then the telephone made immediate voice to voice contact possible. Now computers and the Internet make instant written, oral, and visual contact (via webcam) possible with children and grandchildren all over the world. Cell phones (including the new iPod telephone) with the capacity to connect to the Internet are becoming prolific whereby instant communication between family members and friends is possible.

Increased wellness. Americans as a whole are becoming more aware of the value of proper nutrition and exercise. As a result, they are living longer. Not only is there an explosive increase in the older population, they are healthier than older people of past generations. Now we see more grandparents and great-grandparents per child than ever before in history. Just as the children of Israel

---

2   Faith Popcorn, *The Popcorn Report* (New York: Doubleday, 1994).

were promised that they would see their children's children (Psalm 128:6), today's grandparents, because of their improved health, are just as likely to see their grandchildren on a regular basis. One product of increased wellness is a multiplying of generations at family reunions. In many family reunions there will be great-grandparents, grandparents, adult children, and children. In some families there are even great-great-grandparents who are still able to participate.

Recreation. Recreation is no longer totally home centered. Many family members seek recreational opportunities with organizations that charge membership fees or fees for services. Examples include the YMCA, arcades for computer games, recreation centers with outdoor race tracks, batting cages, and driving ranges. Many churches now provide recreational facilities they call "family life centers" for their members and often these are open to the community as well. Most of these include walking and jogging tracks, swimming pools, racquetball courts, basketball courts, exercise, and other activity rooms. Parties at local restaurants, etc., have replaced the kitchen table and back yard as the setting of choice. Often these styles of recreation have a tendency to segregate the family rather than bring them together. It can also be costly when grandparents feel they need to pay for all of their grandchildren's recreational activities. The positive benefit may be seen in the example of three generations of women (grandmother, mother, and granddaughter) who enrolled in a swimming class at the local community center. They reported that they not only felt healthier, but they had grown closer to each other as a result.

These changes are influencing the way grandparenting is being seen. Grandparents are now learning new ways of holding on to their beliefs while at the same time attempting to understand the different messages grandchildren are getting from television, movies, music and video games. Grandparents are trying to learn new ways of fitting into the lives of their adult children and grandchildren.

In light of these changes and the challenges grandparents face today, the word "career" may be more appropriate for discussing their lives. By definition, career implies a life work. In the appendix of this book you will find a chart identifying and describing unique characteristics of several career types of grandparenting.

Challenges Facing Grandparents in the 21st Century

In the following chapters of this book, we'll discuss and illustrate a variety of grandparenting careers. With grandparenting it is obvious that "one size does not fit all." Grandparents, therefore, have to choose which styles are best for them. Frequently we overhear grandparents speak about getting "stuck." That is, they've decided that grandparenting is an important career for them, but their progress is not what they think it should be. For example, grandparents in blended families do not always get to see the grandchildren as often as they would like. This is often due to the increased number of grandparents in a blended family. It is good if a grandparent in this situation can view being stuck as temporary and move forward with other grandparents by planning for a way that all the grandparents will have time with the grandchildren and also provide a more complete support system for the grandchildren.

Single grandparents face other challenges, such as feeling like a third-wheel. This challenge may already be transforming into an opportunity as we see a majority of family members are choosing to be single. You no longer hear the single person being spoken of as unusual. Instead, single grandparents may enjoy easier travel due to fewer responsibilities at home. It is not uncommon to see married grandparents reach out and invite the single grandparent to join them in celebrating various days and activities of the grandchildren.

Parenting grandchildren, at times, is seen as a burden rather than a blessing because of the added financial responsibilities and lifestyle changes. Yet we see more than 80 million children being raised by their grandparents and 200,000 of these by great-grandparents. Fortunately, there is an increasing number of support groups (both public and private) available for these grandparents and great-grandparents. Stories of grandparents raising grandchildren, once thought unusual, are now seen as typical in most communities. In Derrel's church, for example, a single grandmother raised two of her grandchildren and another couple raised four of their grandchildren and are currently raising one of their great-grandchildren.

Grandparenting college students is certainly a delight. Yet it may be filled with many challenges. A lot of college students may think of the grandparents as "money bags." A significant number of college students are partially or totally sponsored by their grandparents. However, grandchildren most often turn to their grandparents when challenges of one kind or another come up at the university. This may be true because grandparents are generally nonjudgmental and willing to listen. They are likely to respond rather than just react to a particular situation. This way of relating tends to increase the closeness between grandparents and grandchildren in college.

Great-grandparenting is one of the unexpected blessings of the 21st century. A majority of us can anticipate being great-grandparents. Your first response was probably, "I don't believe it." Well, more than 90% of grandparents living healthy lives today will be great-grandparents. Great-grandparenting is allowing us to stay involved with grandparenting for a much longer time. You may not believe this but Ben, who is currently in his mid-sixties (so he says), can now brag about having two great-grandsons, to which he is often heard to exclaim: Wow! What a blessing!

"Surrogate grandparenting" may, to some, be a new term. However, this type of grandparenting has been around since the beginning of humanity. There has always been a neighbor, a teacher, a minister, or even a stranger that steps forward to assume responsibilities and privileges of grandparenting. In recent years several new organizations have sprung up to facilitate the connection between people who want to be surrogate grandparents and children who need a grandparent. One of the best examples is the Foster Grandparent Program. Foster Grandparents is a federal and state program designed to reach out to youngsters with mental challenges, physical challenges, and drug addiction. More than likely there is one in your community. This program was one of Nancy Reagan's favorites. It is so popular that there is a waiting list of people who want to become foster grandparents.

"Grandparenting from a distance" is a phrase used to describe the fact that over half of grandparents do not live close to all of their grandchildren. Only a small percentage of grandparents live with their adult children and grandchildren. In other words, we have few if any "Walton families" left. Most of our grandchildren live some distance from us. For example, one of Ben's grandchildren lives in the same metropolitan area as he, but there is more than fifty miles of city between them. Ben's wife visits their other grandchildren who live in Canada more often than they are able to see the grandchildren who live in the same metropolitan area.

Conclusion

Grandparenting in a technology dominated world can be frightening and challenging. If grandparents remain connected to their adult children and grandchildren, life is not likely to be boring. Today's grandparents and great-grandparents have experienced more rapid, life altering changes than all generations in history. Change, therefore, is not new. How we manage changes and learn to use the technology are the key to accepting and successfully engaging in the new grandparenting careers. As you can see, everything in our grandparenting world is changing. Types of grandparenting and resources such as wireless Internet, digital cameras, text messaging, and iPods, have greatly affected the environment in which we live.

Regardless of our circumstances, we can be effective grandparents if we use the scriptures as our compass. We now live in a world that no longer subscribes to the absolutes of good and bad or right and wrong. The only source of truth that is unchanging yet applies to everyday life is biblical principles. There are some scripture passages you can claim that will help you to become a more effective role model, value carrier, and giver of unconditional love to your grandchildren. The scriptures we list are by no means exhaustive. The primary scripture we claim as our foundation is 2 Timothy 3:16-17. Notice in these verses that the scriptures are said to be our best resource to fully prepare us for our work. Another passage that can assure us of God's thinking about our importance as grandparents is Jeremiah 29:11. Jeremiah simply states that God has a plan for us filled with hope and meaning. Still another is Proverbs 3:5-6. These verses emphasize the importance of trusting and acknowledging the Lord's will and direction in our lives. These and others echo the sufficiency of the scriptures to be our guides in grandparenting.

Take time to read and study each. Follow this time with prayer and thanksgiving that we have as Christians. The exciting thing about being a grandparent in the 21st century can best be captured by the words of Emerson, "Do not go where the path may lead, but go instead where there is no path and leave a trail." Likewise, as Browning says, "Grow old along with me, the best is yet to be…" We believe that is true as well.

Ten Guidelines for Grandparenting in Today's World

1. Acknowledge the honor of being a grandparent.
2. Engage in fun activities and laugh a lot.
3. Explore the different expressions of love and practice them.
4. Build confidences through meaningful communication.
5. Keep confidences by respecting your grandchildren's secrets.
6. Learn and utilize computers and other useful technology.
7. Share your values, including the importance of putting God first.
8. Model grace and forgiveness in your words and behavior.
9. Appreciate your family and its circumstances.
10. Be sensitive to your adult children and grandchildren's schedule.

Prayer

Oh God, as the 119th Psalm says, "Thy Word is a lamp unto my feet and a light unto my path...". Please help me understand, as a grandparent, what I need to know in this complicated and often confusing day in which I live. Please help me know what my children and grandchildren need from me and what I am expected to do in each of my grandparenting careers. Give me wisdom and strength to be the grandparent my grandchildren need as they grow up in this fast changing new world. Amen.

chapter 2

SINGLE GRANDPARENTING

BE GLAD FOR ALL GOD IS PLANNING FOR YOU.
ROMANS 12:12 NLT

THE LORD SAYS, "I WILL GUIDE YOU ALONG THE BEST PATHWAY FOR YOUR LIFE. I WILL ADVISE YOU AND WATCH OVER YOU."
PSALM 32:8 NLT

THERE'S NO TRAFFIC JAM ON THE EXTRA MILE.
ANONYMOUS

Sally, a 34-year-old graduate student, suddenly became a grandparent when her 15-year-old daughter gave birth to a baby girl. Not only was the daughter unmarried, but Sally's husband was killed in an automobile accident two years earlier. Sally is now a single mother and a single grandparent trying to finish rearing her daughter and caring for her baby granddaughter at the same time.

Carl, who is 69 and divorced, is also a grandparent. His wife of 32 years decided that she did not wish to be married any longer. He and his former wife are grandparents to three girls and two boys. Carl spends several hours each week with his children and grandchildren. His former wife lives in a distant city and seldom visits the children.

Betty is a 72-year-old mother of three and grandmother of twelve. Her daughter had two boys by her first husband and married another after a divorce. Her new husband has two girls under the age of 12. Her daughter's sons are 18 and 21. Both are in college. Betty has established a good relationship with all of her grandchildren and she is working hard to establish a strong relationship with the two "bonus" granddaughters and their biological mother and grandparents. Betty's 21-year-old grandson recently began living with his girlfriend who is now pregnant. Betty will soon be a great-grandparent. They have told Betty that they plan to get married "soon." Although they have confided in Betty, neither has told their parents.

These are just a few samples of experiences reported by single grandparents. There are almost as many variations as there are people in this group. Single grandparenting is the fastest growing grandparent group in America today. Some social scientists believe that this is due to the new popularity of singleness. In some cases, singleness is simply a choice, while others may be victims of circumstances beyond their immediate control.

Most likely a majority of grandmothers fall into the single category. We might ask the question, "If this is true, why haven't we heard more about this?" It may be that we have always associated grandparents with older couples and, although we knew some grandparents who were single, we thought of them as exceptions. Also, as one grandmother explained, "It is much easier to associate my singleness with womanhood than it is to attach it to grandparenting." The majority of single grandparents did not choose this label, but rather it became part of their identity due to divorce, remarriage, and/or death. Single grandparenting is becoming more typical because both men and women are choosing to remain single. More than likely you know of several single grandparents in your community.

The question arises, "Is a grandparent known more as a marital status than a parental identity?" It is time for this confusion to be cleared up. We want to do that in this chapter. We will discuss both challenges and opportunities for single grandparents. In addition we will suggest guidelines for increasing the importance and effectiveness of relating to grandchildren and other family members. The biblical passage 2 Corinthians 2:9 can be claimed by single grandparents as a promise from God that will sustain them in every part of their lives.

Defining Single Grandparenting

What is meant by "single grandparenting"? It is similar to an oxymoron such as "jumbo shrimp." Grandparenting has been around since the beginning of humanity, but most do not often think of single grandparenting. Grandparents are assumed, traditionally, to come in pairs. Throughout the scriptures grandparents and grandparenting is spoken of (cf. Genesis 48:11; Job 42:16-17; Proverbs 13:22; Zephaniah 1:1, Titus 2:3-5; 1 Timothy 4:7; 2 Timothy 1:5) while single-status grandparenting is difficult, if not impossible, to find in the Bible. What is true in the scriptures also seems to be true in our culture today. Grandparenting is now being written about more than almost any other position in the multigenerational family. Singleness is also a topic of considerable interest. Yet, "single grandparent," when you put the two terms together, doesn't ring a bell with many.

Single Grandparenting Career/Brand

Regardless of circumstances, single grandparenting requires a second look so that we can determine its "brand" and, at the same time, see if it adequately describes the story about changes in families. While branding is most often associated with business, products, and services, it can also apply to various types of grandparenting as well. Sally is a secretary in a small town law firm. She had to seek employment outside her home when her husband of 24 years suddenly died with a massive heart attack. She had studied secretarial science while a student at the university where she met and married her husband. Both of their children have two small children. Sally has decided that she will not remarry. Most of her time and energy is given to her work and her grandchildren. She is in her mid-forties and looks like she is in her thirties. Few think of her as a grandmother.

One leading marketing specialist suggests eight principles that have been applied by Starbucks and Nike. Three of them are applicable to single grandparenting:

1) Establish "brand" recognition (identity) that is accepted by your grandchildren. The best identity is one that is consistent with God's Word. Proverbs 16:3 promises that your commitment to the Lord will establish your reputation.

The apostle Paul speaks of the importance of keeping your relationship with Christ primary (Galatians 2:20). Sally, the legal secretary/single grandmother mentioned above is very conscious of the impact her lifestyle will have on her children and grandchildren. In addition to her involvement in the Junior League, she is involved in a women's bible study group and sings in the choir at her church.

2) Show your excitement about your relationship with your grandchildren. Imagine the joy expressed in Naomi's heart when the women said, "Naomi has a son." She was, in fact, Obed's single grandmother (Ruth 4:16).

3) Believe that everything about your relationship with your grandchildren matters (Titus 2:7).[3] When Sally was asked to participate in Grandparents' Day at her oldest grandson's school, she baked chocolate chip cookies for the whole second grade. Some of her grandson's classmates remarked that they wished they had a grandmother who could bake good cookies like that.

In order for people to become successful single grandparents, it will be helpful if they develop careers consistent with what they actually are and do. The first step is evaluating what the "single grandparent brand" is. This gives us a better understanding of who they are. The second step is to understand that there are many types of single grandparents. This is not an easy job. Consider three boys in the school yard at recess: One boy says, "My gramps can write a few words on a piece of paper, he calls it a poem, and they give him

---

3   Scott Bedbury, with Stephen Fenichell, *A New Brand World* (New York: Penguin Books, 2002). Bedbury was senior vice-president of marketing at Starbucks and head of advertising for Nike.

fifty dollars." The second boy says, "That's nothing, my granddad scribbles a few words on a piece of paper and they call it a song. He gets a hundred dollars." The third says, "I got you both beat. My papaw scribbles a few words he calls a sermon and it takes at least eight people to collect all the money."

In the past we have generally assumed that if a grandparent was single it was caused by death, desertion, or divorce. In today's world there are other complications that make it harder to understand the full range of issues facing a grandparent who is single. For example, the increased number of blended families has added confusion to the identity of the single grandparent. Blended families bring with them some new relationships which require people to respond to sets of children from two or more families where once there was only one set. The single grandparent is pressured from involvement with the previous family as well as the prospect of integrating new people from a newly established family.

Popular television shows such as those that do "makeovers" of people or houses suggest a strategy that just might work for single grandparents. Bestselling author T. D. Jakes, in his book, *Repositioning Yourself*,[4] says, "You can't have a do-over, but you can reposition yourself and have a make-over." We feel that this is applicable in developing the new brand, single grandparenting.

In the past we have overemphasized the importance grandparents have in the family simply because of their birth or marital relationship. Modern single grandparents will be better known because of their individual identity rather than what the family or society has assigned. In this new brand of grandparenting, people are known and respected more for what they do and who they are than how

---

4 T. D. Jakes, *Repositioning Yourself* (New York: Atria Books, 2007). 23.

their name has been linked to the family in the past. This principle is the first and most important step.

It is important for the new brand, single grandparenting, to be known by three practices:

1) **Listening.** This is one of the most important activities all grandparents can practice as their relationship with their grandchildren develops. Someone said it very well, "How will they ever hear if we don't listen?" As one single grandparent stated it, "When I am tempted to talk about myself and my problems, I bite my tongue. I realize that my grandchildren don't want to hear about all of my problems. Sometimes I think my tongue is becoming 'hamburger meat,' but I try to focus on what my grandchildren want to talk about."

2) Loving grandchildren is not something we have to suggest to grandparents. **Expressing love,** however, in a variety of ways is perhaps the most important action all grandparents can take with their grandchildren. Single grandparents may be tempted to overindulge their grandchildren. Some single grandparents assume that they must make up for the absence of the other grandparent. On the other hand, they may feel like a spare tire in family gatherings, and may choose to spend very little time with their children and grandchildren.

3) **Caring** is more than an emotion; it involves expressions of love that assure grandchildren that their grandparent is truly special. Single grandparents, especially, need to be very careful about "spoiling" their grandchildren. There are a number of reasons grandparents may engage in this practice.

Sometimes this is the result of a feeling of competition with other grandparents for the love and affection of the grandchildren. In other situations it may be simply what they feel is expected. This needs to worked out with the parents of the grandchildren.

Experts call the changes that take place as we live through the days, weeks, and years of our lives "social time." Farmers in the first half of the 20th century, for example, would go to work when it was light enough to see without lights and quit work when they could no longer see. When a farm worker would ask, "What time do we stop working?" The farmer would respond "dark thirty." They did not need a clock or a bell to tell them when to begin or when to quit work. During the past one hundred or so years, factories, trains, busses, airlines, businesses, and schools depended on clocks for their schedules. As a result, we have all become very conscious of time. Traditionally, though, the experiences shared by grandparents and grandchildren were not measured by clocks. A popular preacher and writer said, "God created time; man created watches."[5] In contrast to being "clock watchers," Native American Indians on their reservations follow what some have called "people time." They seem more concerned with visiting and helping family members and neighbors than with time schedules.

One of the ways single grandparents have found to spend unrestricted time with their grandchildren is the grandparent-grandchild seven-day cruise. While on board the ship grandmothers can share a cabin with their granddaughters and participate together in anything that interests them. Another is grandfather-grandson (or granddaughter) fishing trips. Still another is taking a trip on Amtrak across

---

5   Chuck Swindoll, Senior Pastor, Stonebriar Community Church, Frisco, Texas.

the Northwestern part of the United States. Going to a county or state fair, stock show, zoo, museum, etc., can be inexpensive outings as well. Some churches are sponsoring grandparent-grandchildren camping or retreats. Many single grandparents as well as others have found these experiences to be very valuable.

It might be helpful now to think of grandparent time that involves other activities such as family, church, work, and community. While in the past grandparents were not expected to be involved with work, education, and community service, today a majority participate in all these areas. Worship and education are perhaps the only places older grandparents have to be conscious of the clock.

The Single Grandparenting Situation

The question is often raised, "What is it like to be single and a grandparent?" There can be almost as many answers to this question as there are single grandparents. One grandparent answers this question by saying, "All that matters is that I am a grandparent. Whether I am single or married does not affect the love I have for my grandchildren." Another grandmother, answering this question, believes she is a better grandparent since becoming single. In her words, "I am not distracted as much nor do I have to get permission from a spouse to do what I want to do for or with my grandchildren." Still another grandparent speaks of the mix-up that she experiences at church when they are trying to assign her a Sunday school class. She says, "This has been both good and bad. By having membership in two different classes I can choose which one I wish to attend each Sunday. It is much more difficult to stereotype me because of the typical division between singleness and grandparents in a church setting."

It is easy for single grandparents to experience being a different person to many different people. Sometimes this causes grandparents to become frustrated and burned out. At other times this need to be a different person to different people can lead to feeling very tired and angry without really knowing why. If you are a single grandparent who is faced with these types of situations, it is important to take time to inventory your values, i.e., those items that are important to you. Look at how you invest your time on a daily and weekly basis. Stephen Covey, in his book *First Things First*,[6] underscores the importance of adhering to priorities in life. All too often individuals give emphasis to those things which they least value and the least attention to those things they value the most. Covey labels this "the tyranny of the immediate"—that is, feeling that you have to do certain things that are considered essential at the moment, but may not be the most important thing to do. Molly, a single grandmother and a certified nursing aid in a long-term care facility, opted to take the midnight shift in order to be available to her grandchildren during the day. Some would think of the sacrifices of sleep, social activities, and fatigue as factors that would cause most people to decline this option. Such cases as this underscore the selflessness of many single grandparents who are living Covey's principle of "first things first" in everyday life.

Take the professional who works twelve to fifteen hours a day interacting with people of all ages. After a long day at work, he simply wants a place to rest and relax. At the same time he may have received e-mail from a grandchild asking for help on a school project. Even though the grandparent wishes to help, fatigue and mental exhaustion convinces him to respond, "I can't today. Perhaps

---

[6] Stephen Covey, *First Things First* (New York: Fireside, 1994).

tomorrow I can help you."

Still another stumbling block could be the failure to understand what ideas are important to the grandchild. Grandchildren's values often seem so different, especially regarding music, language usage, and things. Grandparents can correct this communication gap by making an inventory of their values, making sure they are theirs and not someone else's. Once the values are identified we suggest that the grandparent make a list of what is most important and what is least important. When the values are prioritized the next step is to decide what things are most important in each of the areas of the grandparent's life and decide what gets first choice and what gets second and so on.

Grandparents do not earn their place of importance in the family. They are accepted just because of who they are. In ancient history grandparents were very important to families. During much of the 20th century grandparents were almost ignored by traditional urban families. Single grandparents were thought of by many as someone you only invited to Thanksgiving and Christmas dinners. They were not expected to make much of a contribution to the well-being of the family. Grandparents, including single grandparents, are now living longer and an increasing number will become great-grandparents. They are healthier than the average grandparent of the past and they are becoming more active in family and community affairs.

Singleness occurs as the result of choices and actions. As a single grandparent, you are more often recognized because of what you do in addition to who you are. The result is that people begin noticing your singleness more than your grandparenting. Single grandparents who know their own values are able to manage this situation much easier when they are more inner-directed than other-directed.

Single Grandparent Stress

One of the causes of stress for single grandparents comes from what other people expect of them, such as how they are expected to behave around others in the family and community. Although the challenges are more visible, there are many benefits to being a single grandparent. Often, however, these benefits are overshadowed by what seems to be an overwhelming number of tasks assigned to the single grandparenting career. Kathryn, for example, feels that she can be a better grandparent to her seven grandchildren because she doesn't have to consult with her husband (who is deceased) about the amount of time and money she spends. At the same time, she is a leader in her church and the chairperson of a women's club that is very active in community service. She is also caring for her middle son who has a handicapped condition as the result of a severe automobile accident. He can only work at part-time jobs and doesn't make enough money to pay his medical bills.

Some single grandparents resist being intimately involved with their grandchildren. Some of the reasons may be anxiety caused by a fear of rejection or being replaced by the grandchild in their adult child's affections. There may also be a fear of being taken advantage of. Many singles do not want their total identity to be grandparent. Others may have a negative feeling about being a grandparent. Some react negatively to the "gushing and gooing" of some grandparents, always showing pictures of their grandchildren. Single grandparents, instead of carrying pictures of their grandchildren, may carry pictures of their pets. Today there is a growing interest in "pet families." Pets can sometimes be a better vehicle single grandparents can use to involve their grandchildren in their lives than cookies and candy making.

Why would a person welcome this identity? Some single grandparents throughout their lives have not been a part of a close family. Now in this new career, there is a special close relationship with their adult children and grandchildren. Others who came from a close family want to give back because their relationship with their grandparents was warm and close. Some experience added pressure when they assume the role of single grandparent because of the death of their spouse. They had a deep love for their spouse and feel that they need to fulfill both the grandmother and grandfather roles.

Unique Expressions of Love by Single Grandparents

Single grandparents have an unlimited repertoire of love expressions at their disposal. Movies and television have limited our vision of what it means to express love. Often, it is only shown as a sexual relationship that is not about real love at all. In our everyday lives we use the term "love" in so many ways. For example, a little girl stayed for dinner at her friend's home. The vegetable was buttered broccoli and the friend's mother asked if she liked it. The child replied, "Oh, yes, I love it." But when the bowl of broccoli was passed she declined to take any. The hostess said, "I thought you said you loved broccoli." The girl replied sweetly, "Oh, yes, ma'am, I do, but not enough to eat it."[7] Some other common expressions of love are, I love French fries; I love Big Band music; I love rock and roll and blues music; I love the beach; I love football; I love Fridays; etc. The ancient Greek language in which the New Testament was written had four different words for love that might provide additional insight into the ways we can express love. All four of these can be

---

7   Michael Hodgin, *1001 Humorous Illustrations for Public Speaking*, (Grand Repids: Zondervan Publishing House, 1994), 267.

defined according to the circumstances and the intentions of the single grandparent. The word "eros" refers to the physical expressions of emotion such as hugging, a pat on the back, a pat on the head, etc. In 1 Thessalonians 2:8 the apostle Paul emphasizes the depth to which a single grandparent may express this type of love: "We loved you so much that we gave you not only God's good news but our own lives too." (TLT) "Storge" referred to the love a parent has for a child and grandchild. A more common word used by the ancient Greeks was "phileo." It referred to friendship and affection. A biblical admonition addresses this type of love: "Love each other with genuine affection and take delight in honoring each other" (Romans 12:10, TLT). "Agape" expresses the intentional process of caring for the welfare of people. It was sometimes translated into English as "charity." Early Christians adopted that reference to love as the type that expresses God's caring for humanity. Grandparents may utilize one or more of these expressions at various times throughout their career. This is one reason it is important to think of grandparenting as a career.

Grandchildren are always watching and often they get a stronger message from what grandparents do than what they say. How you treat a pet, or relate to people of different ethnic backgrounds or stations in life may tell them more about the real meaning of love than anything else you do. Children notice when they hear a grandparent say love words but then fail to follow through with their promises. They also notice when grandparents can be counted on to support them in whatever they are trying to do. As one grandfather said, "Grandchildren have built-in 'bunk detectors.' You may fool them once or twice, but soon they will see through you."

Challenges of Single Grandparenting

Single grandparents may sometimes sense that grandchildren need help and that they are the only ones who can meet the grandchild's need. At other times single grandparents are frustrated when their adult children ask them to provide help for the grandchild when they, the parents, were obviously able to take care of that need. Grandparents in this case may feel that the adult children are taking advantage of their love for the grandchildren.

Some single grandparents recognize that they are serving as role models for grandchildren when their adult children are not doing the job. They may or may not enjoy this assignment. Often single grandparents experience anxiety with this challenge and need help fulfilling this responsibility.

There are times when grandchildren ask their grandparents serious questions dealing with sensitive topics such as sexuality, lifestyles, music, dress, etc. Lifestyle and religious questions may sometimes be difficult to discuss, but it is important for the single grandparent to prepare for them:

- Why do people smoke? Don't they know it is bad for their health?
- What is divorce?
- Do you still love grandma/grandpa?
- Why do you kiss Bob more than mom and dad kiss each other? What is the difference?
- Will you still be my grandparent when you and grandma/grandpa don't live together anymore?
- Can I still come to your house?

- Will you still come to our house at Christmas?
- Why did God take my dad/mom?
- Do animals go to heaven when they die?

Some guidelines that might be helpful:

- Choose your vocabulary carefully when answering children's questions. Be sure to fully understand the question.
- Eye contact is important. Sit and kneel down so you can look into your grandchild's eyes when talking with them.
- Privacy may also be important; they may want to ask questions that are just between the two of you.
- Be sensitive to the grandchild's need for touch. Some may not want you to hold their hands in public or in front of their friends, but they may appreciate a hug in private. Different stages in the grandchild's life dictate what is acceptable or not.
- Be sensitive to the time; they may want to only give you a few minutes rather than an hour.
- You don't have to tell them everything you know. Let them lead the conversation. Are they asking the question because they want to stay up later or do they really want an answer?
- Humor can be a very important tool when dealing with touchy subjects. Be serious when necessary, but remember, you can be *too* serious.
- Music is the universal language, but different generations

have different tastes in music. This may make it difficult to listen to the musical styles you appreciate and still have your grandchildren identify with you.

Consider adopting the practice of an older woman who taught a girl's Sunday school class. She invited all the girls to her house for a dinner. She went to a department store and bought a "boom box" with a CD player. She asked the girls to bring their favorite CD and play their favorite song. She asked each one to explain why they liked that song. She sought first to understand their likes and dislikes before trying to get the girls to listen to the lessons she taught in Sunday school. Single grandparents may learn a lesson from this wise teacher. It would be safe to say that this older woman did not necessarily appreciate the type of music, but communicating with those girls in their own language was more important than her own personal preferences.

Benefits of Single Grandparenting

Often we speak of the challenges of the single grandparent brand and stop there. But there are benefits, too:

- You have a greater opportunity to express your individuality.
- You may have greater flexibility than a married grandparent of scheduling time with the grandchild. Traveling can also be more economical.
- You can create or find an existing single grandparent group you can travel with, learn from, etc. As a single grandparent you might help establish a support group at church, a local social or civic club.

- Single grandparents may be more open to a broader view of life. Don't hesitate, however, to get feedback from adult children and grandchildren regarding your understanding of what a single grandparent is expected to do. They can be one of the best sources of unraveling the tangles from these identities.

- Single grandparents have had a different exposure to the yin and yang of life. Keep a record of the progress you are making in alleviating the unique stresses of single grandparenthood, and identify those individuals who are helpful in affirming single grandparents.

- Single grandparents' thinking style may be more varied (analytical, artistic, etc.).

We are often approached at conferences by older people who have a myriad of questions or stories. Some of them relate to the situations faced by single grandparents. One woman, for example, was recently divorced and currently trying to sort out how she was going to manage her role as a single grandmother. She identified with Dana Haines' poem "Taking the Chance."[8] In that poem, Haines reminded readers of the fact that they were taking chances they never thought they would need to take. As a result, others are seeing who they are and what they are capable of being. She encouraged readers to not wait until tomorrow but live today. Single grandparents are often pressed to move beyond what they thought was their limit and are amazed to realize that they can really do more than they ever thought possible.

---

8   Dana Lee Haines, *Time for Thought*. (Columbus, Georgia: Brentwood Christian Press, 1991), 52.

After reading this chapter, whether you are a single grandparent or fall into one of the other groups, we hope you have come away with a belief that the single grandparenting brand is more important than it is generally considered in society. If you are a single grandparent, we invite you to rethink this expanding career. You have probably heard the old saying, "If you dream it you can do it." As you dream, draw more upon your values than the values of others. Consider the glass to be half-full rather than half-empty. Your spiritual well-being will be a major factor. Think of the confidence, the commitment and the comfort you can have. To those who may not at this time be single grandparents, keep in mind you may become one in the future. We encourage you to reach out and befriend single grandparents, encourage them, welcome them, and most of all be their friend.

If you are a single grandparent, realign your roles in your new single grandparent career, accentuate your positives by celebrating your personhood, potential, passion, and perseverance. These qualities will not only strengthen your determination, but they will also serve as examples to what one can become. This, of course, is especially important to pass on to your grandchildren.

Prayer

Dear Lord, in all my ways I want to follow you and continue to develop my relationship with my grandchildren in such a way as to be a positive witness before them of your love and grace.
Help me to not get in the way of your will in this relationship. Guide me, lead me, and strengthen me as a single grandparent in every path I take. I will continue to honor you and praise you all the days of my life. Amen.

chapter 3

GREAT-GRANDPARENTING

TAKE DELIGHT IN THE LORD AND HE WILL
GIVE YOU YOUR HEART'S DESIRES.
MATTHEW 6:33 NLT

...THEY DELIGHT IN DOING EVERYTHING THE
LORD WANTS; DAY AND NIGHT THEY THINK
ABOUT HIS LAW. THEY ARE LIKE TREES
PLANTED ALONG THE RIVERBANK, BEARING
FRUIT EACH SEASON WITHOUT FAIL.
PSALM 1:2-3 NLT

BE VERY CAREFUL NEVER TO FORGET
WHAT YOU HAVE SEEN THE LORD DO FOR
YOU. DO NOT LET THESE THINGS ESCAPE
FROM YOUR MIND AS LONG AS YOU LIVE!
AND BE SURE TO PASS THEM ON TO YOUR
CHILDREN AND GRANDCHILDREN.
DEUTERONOMY 4:9 NLT

IT AIN'T OVER TILL IT'S OVER.
YOGI BERRA

Picture yourself in the audience at a television quiz show where the contestants are trying to decide which of the two people in front of them is a grandparent and which is a great-grandparent. As the contestants look closely at each candidate, they notice a similarity in dress, posture, and enjoyment of being on TV. Both candidates are articulate, polite, and gracious as the audience applauds their different answers. Fast forward to the end of the show. The panel has selected the wrong person as the great-grandparent. This error is not unusual. Many in our society would have made a similar mistake. The explanation may be found in the change we have experienced because the years no longer separate us. The difficulty in telling the difference between grandparents and great-grandparents is the result of many changes that have taken place over the last twenty years. For example, people of all ages are healthier than in previous generations. Surgeries that replace knees, hips, and other parts of the body reduce the chronic disabilities associated with older ages.

Likewise, with multiple careers, increased economic resources and retirement age being a thing of the past, it is not uncommon to find great-grandparents involved with activities that are similar to those of grandparents. As Christians we are told in Proverbs chapter 3 that by letting one's heart keep God's commandments, the results will provide continued health and vitality (cf. Proverbs 3:1-2, 8).

Better health care, lifelong learning activities, more opportunities to engage in social activities, less physical work, anti-aging beauty products and plastic surgery, and more leisure time—all of these mean it is no longer easy to recognize and separate people of different older generations.

The majority of the readers of this book are probably grandparents. It is most likely that you will become a great-grandparent sooner than you think if you are not one already. A recent story by one of the author's wives underscores that great-grandparenting may include more people than we ever dreamed. The author's wife, "Florence," a grandmother, was visiting in her daughter's home. One evening the whole family, including Florence, was invited to a neighbor's home to meet a great-grandmother. At the close of the evening, after Florence's returning home, one of her grandchildren said, "Bubby, they should call you 'great grandmother'—*all* grandparents are great."

A definition of great includes "much above the ordinary or average; distinguished; having nobility of mind or purpose." Grand includes the concept of "superior rank and status; larger than average; characterized by splendor; distinguished; dignified; excellent; and delightful." A great-grandparent might easily be described as a "grace" parent. People associate the word grace with religion, but it can also be a synonym of great-grandparent. Great-grandparents are so much more than people occupying a position removed by one generation from another. Great-grandparenting has tremendous possibilities as a new career. If you fulfill the new great-grandparent career, you will make a "great grand-slam." In baseball, a grand-slam is when a player hits the ball over the fence when there are runners on every base. A great-grandparent can "hit a grand-slam" by enabling each family member to achieve their ultimate potential, thus bringing about a win for generations to come.

Both authors of this book are relatively young and are currently grandfathers. We enjoy this career; in fact, our grandsons are already making us great-grandparents. Surprised? Yes!—just as you were or will be when you take on the new career of great-grandparenting. In anticipation of this esteemed career, grandparents must begin to equip themselves for the expanded career of great-grandparenting. The differences between grandparenting and great-grandparenting may be much more significant than you realize. Some of the differences include:

- Grandparenting is anticipated by most if not all parents while great-grandparenting is seldom thought of as a possibility in our lives.

- Even though great-grandparents are risk-takers, due to the lack of clarity in expectations they often find themselves in unexplored territory, giving them the opportunity to create new maps about their positions in the ever-changing family.

- Grandparents are more likely to be employed in full-time jobs than great-grandparents who may be sharing a job with another, participating in seasonal work, or offering their job skills to a volunteer organization.

This list of differences is not exhaustive but it does provide evidence that there are valid differences in these two careers.

In this chapter we will identify and discuss the possibilities of great-grandparenting and the relationship with grandparents, grandchildren, and great-grandchildren. In defining contemporary great-grandparents, we must give recognition to a new kind of individual fulfilling this important place. These people have not only learned through their vast experiences over centuries of change, but have learned much about adapting to constantly changing social environments.

That's why today it is different when we speak of great-grandparents. Who would have thought in our lifetime that there would be a separate chapter on great-grandparenting in a grandparenting book? The authors, like most of those in past generations, did not have great-grandparents. They had already died before we were born.

Today, however, many great-grandparents are alive and well, and eager to contribute to the relatively new four- to five-generational family. As is true in societies like ours where change is rapid, a cultural gap exists between where we were twenty years ago and where we are now—especially in regard to great-grandparents. Unfortunately, the gap isn't closing as it should. In this chapter we'll provide a better understanding of the impact of a great-grandparent on the family team. You'll see that, with the mobility, breakdown of families, and ease of being disconnected with families, the great-grandparent can no longer be ill defined. Instead the great-grandparent can fulfill the role of bridging the gaps caused by the various social currents in our society.

In the past when "great-grandparent" identified an individual, our thoughts revolved around an honorary position—that is, there were little or no expectations other than to be present at family reunions and birthday celebrations. Today it means more. As a great-grandparent, you have the freedom to virtually design your own "blueprint" for your new career in the contemporary family.

The cultural great-grandparenting gap is dwindling in size. Those occupying this increasingly important position are pioneering the way for more useful and practical roles in today's family.

Historically you could almost describe the family in "cookie-cutter" manner. Each individual accepted certain behavioral expectations, few questions were asked. There was little or no competition between and among generations, and little thought was given beyond the first level of grandparenting. Now the family scene has changed where few, if any, willingly accept the behavioral expectations associated with the family of the past. Some only remember the great-grandmother sitting in a rocking chair, reading her Bible and humming a hymn such as "Amazing Grace" "The Old Rugged Cross" or "How Great Thou Art."

Great-grandparenting—and indeed grandparenting at all levels—involves competition with gift-giving and special invitations to family gatherings as well as cooperation within and among generations. Geropsychiatrist Gene Cohen, in his book *Creative Aging*,[9] discusses the importance of employing creative aging techniques to facilitate the search for a more fulfilling and satisfying later life. To encourage the search, it is helpful to view the family composition in a way that acknowledges the individuality of each member. Greater possibilities exist for aligning great-grandparents' unique attributes with the increasing tasks associated with family. Great-grandparents of today are in a position to write their own scripts for relating to at least two different sets of grandchildren as well as a multitude of parents.

Family positions have been designed through trial and error over the years to meet and fulfill responsibilities necessary for a healthy family group. Most of these tasks can be seen in the first few levels of Maslow's hierarchy of needs, which is illustrated by a pyramid. The basic needs are illustrated at the bottom of the pyramid and the spiritual needs at the top. The new great-grandparent career, while continuing to be engaged with the basic or deficiency needs, is free to incorporate the higher level or growth needs of people. It is assumed that those upper level needs are never completely met but are lifelong challenges. Two of those that are particularly appropriate for great-

---

[9] Cohen, Gene D., *The Creative Age* (New York: Avon Books, 2000).

grandparents is the need to become all one can be (self-actualization) and to achieve a condition of "gerotranscendence." Most people are not familiar with gerotranscendence, which both Abraham Maslow (famous humanistic psychologist who is best known for his theory of a hierarchy of needs in human development) and Erik Erikson (famous for suggesting eight stages of psychosocial development of human life) added to their developmental schemes toward the end of their careers. Gerotranscendence refers to a person's ability to achieve a high level of spirituality. Great-grandparents, at this level, would have incorporated their spirituality into every aspect of their lives.

Another exciting possibility of your all new great-grandparenting career is the perspective that your contributions will not simply be assigned "tasks" but will be characterized by flexibility and increased insight about caring. At this stage, you understand the importance of patience and perseverance. Your time schedule permits more emphasis on love, nonjudgmental responses, and being a friend that transcends generational differences.

Great-grandparents today can provide the family continuity that has often lost its links to its roots. When more people are interested in discovering their roots, who is most able to share them with the children, grandchildren, and great-grandchildren? Consider some of the life experiences and characteristics of today's great-grandparents:

- Strong work and values, ethic.
- Strong attachment to the environment.
- Respect for public leaders and a sense of obligation to do their part in keeping this country free. They lived through more wars than any other generation.

- The influence of individualism in their lives.
- The ability to make much out of little. They lived through the great Depression.
- The strong pull toward their independence.
- Relying on others only when it was absolutely necessary.
- Frugality characterized their lifestyles. They did not have credit cards and would only borrow money to put in the crops or buy property.
- Faith was central in their lifestyle.

These characteristics are more prevalent in the leading edge "Builder" generations (born before 1942) than the trailing edge (born 1942-1946) or Boomer great-grandparents (born after 1946). We must not forget that much of our life is characterized by a contradiction between our priorities and values. Too often what is least important is at the top of our priorities and what is most important ends up at the bottom. The observations we have made lead us to believe that great-grandparents have repositioned their priorities according to their values. As a result, their top priorities appear to be deeper relationships, more unconditional love, less judgment, and more confidence in the generations following them.

These great-grandparents have a broader perspective of the family. They have a more complete picture. If anyone is qualified to be a change agent it is the great-grandparent. They have not only witnessed change, their generation has contributed to more radical changes in technology and culture than any other generation in the history of the human race. They have proven their adaptability by the numerous adjustments to technology, economics, travel, government, education, and the globalization of communication. For the most part, they grew up in a society where relationships represented the end of their involvement instead of a means to an end.

Stereotypes of Great-Grandparents

Great-grandparents face discrimination based upon myths and stereotypes. Some of those stereotypes are:

- All great-grandparents are frail, inactive, and lack mobility and vitality for the everyday tasks of life.
- Great-grandparents are part of the oldest-old age group.
- Great-grandparents are out of touch with the "real world."
- They have an inability to learn and integrate technology into their lifestyles.
- They only have friends in their age group.
- They are not interested in the future.
- They only think and talk about the past.
- They lack involvement outside the family.
- They are rigid and respond negatively to suggestions for change.
- They want to be spectators rather than participators.
- They are dependent rather than inter-dependent.
- They are consumers of services rather than providers.

Overcoming the stereotypes mentioned above is not easy. Many of these stereotypes arose from people's experience with a limited number of people labeled as great-grandparents or the "oldest old."

Of course, this leads to overgeneralization—that is, what you see and experience with a few is characteristic of all in a group. Here are some suggestions for fighting back to begin the process of removing these stereotypes:

- Be yourself.
- Don't define yourself solely in terms of your age.
- Develop friendships with people from other generations.
- Don't be passive; be assertive in who you are as a great-grandparent.
- Educate those who continue to keep these stereotypes alive.
- Pray for those who entertain these stereotypes. Ask God to give them understanding and you patience in correcting their misperceptions.
- Enlist others to join in the battle of destroying these stereotypes.

How to Become a Successful Great-Grandparent

Learn to age well. Aging well is a choice. When learning takes place, there is change in attitude and behavior. Read Arthur Gordon's book *A Touch of Wonder*.[10] Many of his suggestions will help you see that aging well has to do more with lifestyle than anything else. Keep in mind you don't just learn once. With the large amount of research on aging well, it will be easy for you to remain current on all the latest ways you can design and live a full and complete life. Likewise claim the promises God has given us and do God's will by

---

10   Gordon Arthur, *A Touch of Wonder* (New York: Penguin Group, 1974).

obeying 1 Thessalonians 5:18, "No matter what happens, always be thankful for this is God's will for you who belong to Christ Jesus" (NLT).

Learn from the successes of other great-grandparents. One of the most economical ways to be successful in great-grandparenting is to seek out other great-grandparents who have been innovative and adaptable to changing situations, which almost always occur in a multigenerational family. One great-grandparent was saddened by the fact that her great-grandson was not interested in giving her a big hug. This disappointing behavior occurred quite frequently. When telling another great-grandparent about her desire to have hugs from her grandson, the great-grandparent she was speaking to interrupted her quickly and said, "Sometimes we try too hard. We might push ourselves too fast on these little ones. I have learned to smile, to listen, be patient, and let the great-grandchildren do these things, like hugs, as they desire." The great-grandparent, having a desire for hugs from her great-grandson, applied what her friend suggested. Within a month the great-grandson was responding to his great-grandmother's smile, warmth, and the attention she was giving him while he played in the back yard. Now he hugs her so tight that at times she feels she can't breathe. She says, "This is okay. I have what I wanted most."

Avoid age grading. Don't permit anyone to categorize you in terms of how many years you have lived. Instead, encourage them to see you for what you've done with your life, how you look and feel, and how much you've grown in important areas like spirituality and life experiences. I remember a great-grandmother who was known as a Christian being very special at a camp in the Hill Country of Texas. Her primary duties involved preparing desserts for both lunch and dinner. The campers especially liked her desserts. They often said, with a big smile on their faces, "Great-grandmamma, your desserts are as sweet as you are." She not only helped with the meals, but played an important part in drawing attention to the wonders God created in his universe. It was not uncommon to find this great-grandmother sitting on a picnic bench with a dozen or more campers, ages nine to eleven, listening to her stories about the outdoors. As night approached, she would encourage the campers to be still and listen to the wind as it moved through the dense forest. One camper said, "You know, great-grandma, if you had not told me to listen I would have missed one of the most amazing sounds I have ever heard." Before you knew it, she was pointing toward the sky, having the children notice a falling star. Prior to her saying goodnight to all of her "great-grandchildren," she reminded them of the fact that only God could create a world (the outdoors) as they experienced it that day.

Network with all age groups. Make an effort to develop friendships with people younger and older than you. By relating to different age groups you increase your resources, multiply your opportunities and enrich your life. Don't limit yourself only to friendships with people the same age as you.

Be computer literate. Your ability to communicate can be vastly increased by use of the computer and all of its assets. Don't be afraid to learn something new. Enroll in the senior network that is available throughout the world. Its members are willing to teach you how to e-mail, send pictures, and search websites to help you stay connected and grow in understanding of your grandchildren and great-grandchildren.

Realize you have a story worth telling. Celebrate your memories; they are sacred. You have a greater variety of life experiences than anyone else in your family. Those stories are a significant part of who you are and they can be meaningful to your children, grandchildren, and great-grandchildren. Derrel, one of the authors, for example, enjoys telling his grandchildren about winning a radio talent contest at age fifteen, and performing on a stage in a high school auditorium near Memphis, Tennessee. That same night there was another fifteen-year-old who performed on the same stage. He was from Memphis and his name was Elvis. Derrel usually grins and says, "Neither of us was famous at the time, but that changed in just a few years. Now, everybody knows his name."

Become a "wisdom giver." Wisdom is the ability to take what you know and make good decisions in new situations. Sharing your faith and values with your family, when they are willing to listen, allows them to benefit from your experiences and knowledge. Recognize that you *do* have wisdom. Make an inventory of your life experiences and your spiritual formation and be prepared to share them with your family when the time is right. Review the wisdom literature in the Bible such as Proverbs and Ecclesiastes so you can gain insight into how to understand your own values and thus your wisdom. We have discussed some of the scriptures you can pass on to your great-grandchildren at the appropriate time. A few are: Psalm 56:10, 11, 13; Psalm 119:103; 1 Corinthians 9:27; Proverbs 1:7; "The fear of the Lord is the beginning of knowledge..."; Matthew 20:27, "And whoever will be chief among you, let him be your servant." John 11:25-26, "Jesus said unto her, I am the resurrection and the life..." Romans 5:8, "But God demonstrated his love toward us in that while we were yet sinners, Christ died for us."

Build a solid spiritual foundation. Keep growing in your faith.

Read your Bible, spend time in prayer, get involved in the practice of your faith. Help people who are less fortunate. Jesus, in Matthew 7:24-27, teaches that a solid foundation rests upon reading God's word and putting his instruction into practice. Those who don't are like the builder who built on shifting sand. The result will be catastrophe when times get tough.

Control stress and don't let stress control you. Some stress is helpful; too much stress is harmful both mentally and physically. One manifestation of excessive stress is worry. Be leery of "all or nothing" thinking. Philippians 4:6-7, "Don't worry about anything, instead pray about everything. Tell God what you need and thank him for all he has done. If you do this you will experience God's peace, which is far more wonderful than the human mind can understand. His peace will guard your heart and mind as you live in Christ Jesus" (NLT). Great-grandparents have experienced times when they could not have it all and they survived. Anger and unforgiveness can be devastating stressors. Feeling that you must please everyone is not only wrong but it is emotionally damaging. Thinking that you must continue all of the old family traditions can be too heavy a burden. Allow other family members to assume some of the responsibility for things like Thanksgiving or Christmas dinners. The most important thing is your presence.

Get out of your comfort zone. Don't be afraid to try some new things. Sample some new foods, different clothes, hair styles or music. This recommendation is critical not only to developing a better relationship with your great-grandchildren, but it will also contribute to your own mental wellness. It is well known that habits can develop into "ruts" and ruts make us bored, which can make us more vulnerable to depression. As you make an effort to move beyond your comfort zone, begin by taking small steps. Increase your steps as you gain confidence in attempting new activities.

Continue to play—avoid becoming a couch potato. Keep your childlike wonder and playfulness. Get involved and have fun with group activities like walking, swimming, traveling, fishing, dancing, cards, games, golf, miniature golf, bowling or shuffleboard. When you play, consider playing with others rather than just sitting alone and watching television.

This suggestion also applies to your mental activities. Often due to habit we respond to people with the same answers we've used for more years than we would like to remember. Try some "mental aerobics" such as reading, crossword puzzles, Sudoku (a number game) or select a book on mental aerobics at your local library and choose the activity you like best. You'll begin to see a lot of your grandchildren's thoughts and activities in a different light. And it will stretch your mind and thinking to contribute to your own mental wellness.

Be an encourager. Encouraging a grandchild is a priceless gift. Grandchildren of all ages need to be encouraged to follow their dreams, seek new adventures and to know that they are okay in terms of who they are. In other words, to be an encourager you must set judgment aside, give more emphasis to unconditional love, and let your grandchildren know you are with them every step of the way.

Look for humor in life events. There is nothing that brings two people closer than a good laugh. Keep a sense of humor in the forefront when communicating with your grandchildren. Don't be afraid to share a joke, a funny story, a cartoon, or a hilarious moment in your life. A grandchild, for example, when the teacher asked where her grandmother lived, very innocently said, "At the airport. Every time grandmother comes to visit us we pick her up and take her back to the airport."

Conclusion

Great-grandparenting is becoming one of the fasting growing new trends in American culture. No longer is the prestigious position considered to be a "roleless role." On the contrary, a large portion of the grandparent population living today can expect to become great-grandparents, thus opening up a new second career of grandparenting. Some people who have been both grandparents and great-grandparents believe that great-grandparenting is much more fun. As a great-grandparent, you may begin this career much earlier than you ever imagined. So you may want to reread this particular chapter more than once. Let the words and thoughts in this chapter be the beginning of your search in discovering the kind of great-grandparenting career you want.

By the way, don't be surprised if you pick up a revised copy of this book and we have added a chapter on great-great-grandparenting. Colossians 2:6-7, "And now, just as you accepted Christ Jesus as your Lord you must continue in obedience to him. Let your roots grow down into him and draw nourishment from him so you will grow in faith, strong and vigorous in the truth you were taught. Let your lives overflow with thanksgiving for all he has done" (NLT).

Prayer

Heavenly Father, you have blessed me with long life, given me more opportunity to serve you. As a great-grandparent I pray that my testimony will extend to all generations in my family. I especially ask for your grace and guidance in my efforts to teach, to care, and to love my great-grandchildren. My deepest desire is for them to know and understand John 3:16. Thank you for providing me with what I need to fulfill your will in leading my great-grandchildren to have Christ-centered lives. Amen.

chapter 4

GRANDPARENTING IN BLENDED FAMILIES

> DON'T JUST PRETEND THAT YOU LOVE OTHERS. REALLY LOVE THEM...LOVE EACH OTHER WITH GENUINE AFFECTION AND TAKE DELIGHT IN HONORING EACH OTHER.
> ROMANS 12:9-10 NLT

> WHEN YOU COME TO A FORK IN THE ROAD, TAKE IT.
> YOGI BERRA

Over one third of grandparents in North America would be included in what most writers refer to as "step-grandparents." That is, their children marry a person who already has one or more children. Ready or not, this situation inducts them into the "blended family" population. We might liken a blended family situation to having a rock in your shoe. We've all experienced having a foreign object in our shoe that makes it difficult to walk. Most of us find that the solution is simply to remove the shoe, take the rock out, and put the shoe back on and before you know it you're ready to go. It may not be so easy, however, in the case of the step-grandparent in a blended family. The "rock" in this family dynamic may be history, conflict, or confusion about who is in what position and to what role they should play. Though it may appear complicated, blended families with some encouragement and help can remove any rocks that may keep them from becoming the family they desire to be. A significant number of families have been able to make this transition with little or no difficulty.

While a significant amount of literature has been written about blended families, very little of it has been about step-grandparents. The Bible does not mention step-grandparenting specifically. In the book of Ruth, Naomi would technically be a step-grandparent. However, in Jewish tradition, the child born to Ruth (Naomi's daughter-in-law) and Boaz (Naomi's kinsman redeemer), was considered to be Naomi's own grandchild.

In this chapter we hope to highlight some of the challenges and positive outcomes of grandparenting in the blended family context. The term step-grandparenting is not consistent with the idea of building a blended family. Neither does "blended family" cover all the facets of extended family relationships when the parties are not biologically related. Normally the term blended refers to bringing together two or more elements in such a way that they become fused together as one. Perhaps, "cograndparenting" might be a better description of the relationship. Cograndparenting implies that the family units brought together retain their uniqueness, but find ways to work together for the benefit of the grandchildren as well as the rest of the family.

Realities of Cograndparenting

Let's begin with a wonderful story experienced by one of the authors, in his desire to blend two families together. Derrel shares that a lifelong wish is that he could have granddaughters. He already had two fine grandsons, he still desired a granddaughter and it appeared that there would be no other grandchildren in his life. That all changed, however, when his daughter announced she was marrying a man who had two young daughters. Finally he was going to experience the joy of relating to two little girls who became his instant granddaughters. Derrel's daughter told her new stepdaughters, ages five and eight, that they were going to have two "bonus grandparents." The oldest said, "Goody! Two more grandparents to spoil us." The girls chose the names "Bonus Granddaddy" and "Bonus Grandmommy" for their new step-grandparents. The transition of including two new granddaughters into the family has been a smooth one. The girls, after four years, have accepted their new bonus grandparents as vital parts of their family. Derrel and his wife, Janis, developed a positive relationship with their new son-in-law almost immediately. The relationship between the step-grandparents and the girls' biological mother has also been very positive.

Ben, another of the coauthors, is experiencing the joy of being a cograndparent in a blended family. In his situation one of his wife's grandsons had no living grandfathers. Even though Ben and his family were of one faith persuasion and his wife another, this did not interfere with the desire of his wife's daughter to have him as a grandfather of her children. One of the first grandchildren to call Ben on Father's day was Michael, just over four years old. He called to wish his "new grandfather" a happy Father's day. Although his wife's other children have both grandparents alive,

Ben has successfully blended into their families as well. Likewise he has been able to continue his relationship with his biological grandchildren. It is interesting that some of his biological grandchildren call his wife "Bubby," a title of endearment to one who is respected and loved. On numerous occasions the grandchildren from Ben's side as well as his wife's side enjoy meeting for outings and to experience the pleasure of having additional playmates.

In another situation, a divorce and remarriage join two families together. In the beginning the newly married couple assumed everyone would accept one another and continue to have a strong family foundation. It didn't quite happen as expected. The new husband had a daughter who was very close to him and to her biological mother as well. Over the years the daughter began to feel guilty about spending time with her father and his new wife. The guilt came from the close attachment that developed with her mother since the divorce. The daughter married and she and her husband had two children. Outwardly you would have never guessed that this blended family was unstable. Formality was observed on special occasions such as birthdays, Christmas, and anniversaries; greetings and positive conversations were exchanged. However, the "little things" that speak louder than words were lacking. The father was always the one who had to initiate telephone calls and invitations for dinner and recreational activities. It seemed as if the daughter was simply following a script to avoid confrontation with her father, giving her less stress and the opportunity to invest the majority of her time with her husband's parents. In this situation there was a lack of balance resulting in the father grieving over "the loss of his daughter" and the lack of opportunity to interact with his grandsons.

People have become cograndparents as young as 28 years of age. In many if not most of these situations, the teen-age daughter became involved with a man who already had one or more children. It is not unusual for people to become cograndparents or co-great-grandparents when they are in their eighties or nineties. People who become cograndparents are, most often, already biological grandparents to one or more grandchildren. These new grandchildren are sometimes referred to as "instant grandchildren."

There are at least three ways grandparents become cograndparents:

1) When your adult child marries a person who already has one or more children. The grandchild already has biological grandparents. Your adult child has to relate to those layers of relationships as well as maintain a relationship with you and your parents, siblings, and other extended family members.

2) When your son or daughter, who already has one or more children, marries a person who does not have children. This is the reverse of number one. You must relate to the new spouse and his other extended family.

3) Your adult child and spouse adopt a child in a situation where the biological parents and grandparents are known. The grandchild also has biological grandparents and extended family that are not legally related.

In recent years more has been written about the emotional complications of artificial insemination where the sperm is drawn from a sperm bank. In some cases though, the donor signs a release allowing the child to know who the "father" is. In many cases the donor does not desire any relationship with the child that is born by this method. This often presents a dilemma for biological grandparents. One donor could be the biological father of 20 or more children and the grandparents have no knowledge of their grandchildren. In this situation, the sperm donor and the mother are not known to each other and the grandparent relationship is totally with the daughter and the grandchild.

Relationships with Your Child's New Spouse

Affirming your acceptance of the "new" spouse of your adult child can go far to enhance future relationships with your grandchildren. Ideally, all parties involved should make the effort to build relationships, but it may be necessary for you to take the initiative.

Some cograndparents have made the mistake of assuming that it doesn't matter what the new son- or daughter-in-law thinks; they assume their relationship with their own adult child is stable and unbreakable. In reality, strained relationships with the new spouse can cause a great deal of hurt and even separation, thus limiting relationships with grandchildren. Sandra, an African American grandmother, did not like the man her daughter married. She though he was a lazy man who would only work long enough to get enough money to buy cigarettes and booze. Her daughter Melissa had two children, a boy and a girl, whom the grandmother loved dearly. She, however, did not try to hide her negative feelings from her new son-in-law and his parents. Soon after the marriage, her daughter, son-in-law, and grandchildren moved to another state. The daughter's new husband did his best, but could not seem to keep a job. Sandra's daughter took a job and neighbors cared for the children. Sandra tried to get Melissa to leave her husband and move back home where she could help take care of the grandchildren. Melissa would not listen and was determined to make her marriage work. Over the years Sandra grieved because she could not see and care for her grandchildren.

Another issue arises at the point when care giving is needed for one or more grandparents and their adult children feel responsible for coming to their aid. This can create a significant burden for the blended family. If the spouse of the adult child has a good relationship with the grandparent everything can be easily worked out. If, on the other hand, relationships have been stressful, there can be a significant amount of difficulty. Gerocounselors who have been trained to work with older families may provide coaching services that will help the families to find workable solutions to these issues.

Relationships with Other Cograndparents

Grandparents in blended families are trying to fill positions in the family that were traditionally created for biological grandparents. With the increase of divorce in our society, efforts are being made to include more people in the traditional grandparent position. So it is necessary to develop new types of relationships that will create a harmony in the family that will benefit the grandchildren. Primarily, these new relationships begin with new spouses and "instant grandchildren." However, each part of the blended family brings an extended family into the picture. Some have erroneously said, "I am not marrying her family." The fact is, we do marry the person and all his or her relatives. They have had a part to play in our development and will continue to have an influence in our lives.

Often, in blended families, when new grandchildren are born they are considered half-brothers or half-sisters to the existing grandchildren. If cograndparents are not sensitive to the impact they have on their grandchildren, they can cause significant stress on the developing relationships in the blended family. For example, when a new baby is born into the family, it can cause emotional stress if a grandparent says to the grandchildren, "You know, don't you, that baby girl is your half-sister? She is not totally your sister like you are to your brother." Or, when it comes time to naming the new baby, stress can increase when one grandparent insists on having the baby named after her or his side of the family. Cograndparents could benefit from agreeing to make only suggestions that are requested, rather than volunteering them.

The "playing field" for a blended family changes considerably and the rules governing family life may need to be modified. This task is easier than we might think. Often the cograndparents are the ones that may be the most open minded and serve as examples to the rest. Grandparents, for the most part, have lived long enough to realize what priority best fits the family. Keep in mind the goal of the blended family should be to develop compatibility with each member. To do this, there needs to be acceptance and respect for each individual as a member of the family. We must also be willing to forgive the small infractions of any rules that the family may have established.

If as cograndparents you will draw upon your faith, no matter what it may be, you will find important principles that will help guide you in those important relationships. For example, both the Old and New Testaments instruct believers to be obedient to God's commands, including loving one another and sharing with the generations following them. John 13:34 is a clear message from Jesus to Christians about how we are to relate to each other: "So now I am giving you a new commandment: Love each other. Just as I have loved you, you should love each other" (NLT). The type of love Jesus was commanding is not just an emotional feeling, but a type that is always trying to do what is best for one another.

Although it may not be necessary to become good friends with other grandparents in your grandchildren's life, it will be important to their well-being if you can maintain a civil relationship with them. The apostle Paul's instructions apply here: "Do your part to live in peace with everyone, as much as possible" Romans 12:18 (NLT). Most grandparents from each side of the blended family will make efforts to demonstrate their love for their grandchildren. The idea of cograndparenting suggests that each set of grandparents makes an effort to work together for the good of the blended family. For example, some cograndparents have chosen to invest in a shared housing arrangement whereby they live in the same building or in the same retirement complex and look out for one another.

Relationships with Extended Family

In the typical family there are more than parents and grandparents. Uncles, aunts, and cousins play a significant role in the traditional family. When a new blended family is formed, the full range of extended families is brought together. Cograndparents must also strive to include these extended families in their circle of acquaintances. They can be resources in times of family conflict. They can also be negative influences in times of family stress. For example, Cousin Loretta was very quick to volunteer her opinions about children and their relationships with other families. She very sharply criticized the gifts her mother- and father-in-law gave to her children. She said that she knew for a fact that they paid more for the gifts they gave to his children.

Guidelines

With the variety of relationships that exist in blended families, it is helpful to have guidelines, not rules, which can apply in almost any situation. The guidelines presented are not exhaustive but provide a beginning to help you contribute to a healthier blended family.

- Recognize the importance of cograndparents in the multigenerational family.
- Accept that there are differences when two families are joined together.
- Give the grandchildren the highest priority in the family.
- Acknowledge the gifts and talents of each grandparent and how they can complement other grandparents in the blended family.
- Practice forgiving one another when feelings are hurt as a result of not being including in such things as frequency of visits, invitations to family affairs, or being overlooked on special occasions.
- Seek common interests with cograndparents. Common interests may be the best means of bridging or overcoming difficulties in blending families.
- Establish yourself as a "safe" person and create safe situations for the blended family. You create a safe place by being a peacemaker, a neutral ear, and not becoming an emotional drain in family interactions.
- Rely on your spiritual resources to negotiate difficult times in the blended family.

- Discover humor in unexpected, unique, and even challenging times that may arise in the blended family.
- Accept your cograndparents as colleagues on the team. They can be helpful to your children and grandchildren, especially when they are experiencing many changes in their lives.
- Respect family histories and consider their importance in initiating new histories for the blended family.

Some of the events in the lives of families that can lead to trouble in our relationships with blended families are gift-giving at Christmas and birthdays, celebrations, weddings, graduations, and funerals. It would be helpful to discuss these things with our families when they are not an issue at the moment. Problems often pop up when someone does not understand the traditions or expectations surrounding these important events. Carl, for example, always gave each of his grandchildren a silver dollar for each year of their lives on their birthdays. His son married a woman who had three children who were six, eight, and ten years of age. His daughter had two children, thirteen and fourteen years old. His son's wife became upset when she noticed that Carl gave his daughter's children more money than he gave to each of her children. She had not been told that Carl's practice was to give each a silver dollar representing each year of their lives. When her husband, Carl's son, explained Carl's tradition, she understood and changed her attitude.

Gift giving. Cograndparents often end up comparing the amount and quality of gifts they give to their grandchildren. This is a trap we need to avoid. You should give gifts according to the needs of the grandchildren. Do not let guilt, competition or financial resources drive your gift giving: by doing so, you will never feel like your gift is good enough. Remember that a gift is given to please the grandchild rather than other members of the extended family. In any type of family there is a certain amount of competition that goes along with gift giving. We have learned from the stories of many adult grandchildren that the gifts they value most have been pictures of the family and stories about their family history. Assurances that their grandparents are praying for them every day and that they can count on their grandparents to be available when they are needed are truly the best gifts.

Celebrations, weddings, and funerals. Willingly cooperate and lend a hand with special events such as weddings, graduations, retirements, birthdays, baby showers, births of great-grandbabies, and the loss of family members to death. Sometimes it is financial help that is needed; at other times it is simply helping with the arrangements and serving the guests. It's true that such events can be awkward. If this is the case it gives you an opportunity to set a good example for your grandchildren by rising to the occasion and being cooperative.

Getting help. An increasing number of professional counselors, social workers, and family therapists are developing expertise in working with issues faced by older families, including a variety of grandparenting situations. Most of the time grandparents can draw upon their experiences and their faith to deal with whatever difficulties they encounter. However, there are times when the situation calls for someone outside the blended family to help resolve the conflict.

Prayer

Our heavenly Father, lover of all people, we thank you and praise you for the opportunity to experience family once again. Help us to see all our grandchildren as ours to love, encourage, help, and pray for. We want to contribute harmony to this newly established family. We truly desire to magnify the love of Christ in all our ways. May your presence always be with us and give us wisdom in all our decisions so that our Savior may be magnified and glorified in all that we do. Amen.

chapter 5

Grandparents Raising Grandchildren

> Only be careful, watch yourselves closely so that you do not forget the things your eyes have seen or let them slip from your heart as long as you live. Teach them to your children and to their children after them.
>
> Deuteronomy 4:9 NIV

> Raising my three grandchildren turned out to be the biggest blessing of my life. My only regret is that I felt so stressed at the time that I didn't relish each moment.
>
> Barbara M.

One of the most notable demographic changes in our society today is the large number of grandparents raising their grandchildren. As a gerontologist, it is my good fortune to work with many individuals in this situation. I call them *"GRGs"* (Grandparents Raising Grandchildren).

It may come as a surprise to many that Oklahoma has one of the highest percentages of GRGs in the nation. We have responded accordingly by providing a vast number of services, including written materials and an annual spring and fall conference. These conferences are incredible experiences. They offer lots of speakers, great resource information, and free counseling. The biggest benefit, in my opinion, is that it affords these grandparents an opportunity to talk about their situations. And, do they let it all out! The stories are amazing, each one different and unique.

At the close of a conference a few years ago, a man came up to one of the speakers and told of the need to either take his grandchildren in or let them go to foster homes. He said, "I felt that it was my responsibility and therefore I had no choice. There was only one right thing to do. Take those children in and raise them. I was on a Social Security income and needed to find a job because of the added cost. It has been difficult, but I know I have to do it. It is important to me that they be raised in a godly home. I believe that God is going to provide a way for me to earn the money."

A Mindset Change

Over the years, I've collected these stories and have kept solid notes. I would frequently brainstorm with other colleagues about what could be done to better these GRG situations. We've tried many innovative ideas like support groups, online chat rooms and telephone buddy systems. We've tackled the issue legislatively, putting into place mechanisms that help grandparents legally. This was certainly effective and appreciated. But we were still missing that "something"—a key ingredient that could radically improve the GRG experience.

One day, I was visiting with Norma, a dear friend of mine and a grandmother who had been raising her grandson for nearly 13 years. She is a real veteran—a seasoned GRG. During our conversation, I told her I was contributing a chapter to a forthcoming book on grandparenting and I wanted to share a fresh idea or perspective relative to grandparents raising grandchildren. I asked her, given all her experience, what she thought would be the most effective thing we could tell GRGs? Her answer surprised me. And, as it turns out, I believe it is *the key* to bettering the GRG situation. She said, "More than anything, we need to convince GRGs that it's a matter of mindset. Like so many others, when I first became the guardian for my grandson, I changed everything. I thought I had to. I was in scramble mode and never paused to think through the situation. I panicked. In looking back, it cost me my marriage, my job and my health. I realize now that it didn't have to be that way. If I had developed a plan, ensured that I met my own needs, things would have turned out fine." 2 Timothy 3:16 in the Phillips Translation supports her in this conclusion: "All scripture…is useful for teaching the faith and correcting error, for resetting the direction of a person's life, and training in good living."

What a fresh, unique and honest perspective! It struck me how similar her comment was to a previous program we had developed to help family caregivers called *Replenishing the Caregiver*. In that program, we placed 100% of the attention on the care provider rather than the care receiver. In many cases this was a middle aged individual caring for an aging parent or an older adult caring for a spouse. For so many years in this country, we gauged the success of a caregiver relationship solely on how well cared for the recipient was and if all his or her needs were being met. This often came at great sacrifice for the caregiver. Startling research indicated that some caregivers were dying before their care recipients. Others would often see their own health worsen. Why? Because these caregivers felt that to honorably perform their role, they had to give it all. They had to stop their own lives, put their own desires and ambitions on hold, and focus entirely on caring for their loved one. Sadly, the end result was often having two people (both provider and recipient) at risk instead of just one.

The answer? Encourage caregivers to first meet their own needs. The commonly used analogy is what happens during a flight emergency. When the masks drop from the ceiling, you are instructed to put your mask on first and then aid a dependent with their mask. Airline safety experts realized how important it was for you to be taken care of first. Putting your mask on first enables you to help others. If you focus on the dependent first and you panic or something malfunctions, you have now jeopardized the well-being of two individuals and doubled the risk.

A tension exists between what society expects of the care provider and what the provider needs to do to be effective in the long run. It is our opinion that better quality parenting will be the result of the grandparent maintaining as high a level of physical, mental, and spiritual wellness as possible. For this to happen, adequate support is necessary in the family and the church. This would be consistent with what Jesus taught by his life and his words as well.

Through the *Replenishing the Caregiver* program many family caregivers reconfigured their priorities. In keeping with the message of the 23rd Psalm, they implemented respite into their lives. They focused on their own well-being, exercised more, ate healthier foods, reconnected with friends, restarted past hobbies, and renewed their own private time with God. They looked beyond the present and envisioned a more balanced future. No, it wasn't easy. It took planning, lots of communication and a willingness to work through difficult issues. Most importantly, it called for a mental adjustment. They had to accept that what they were doing wasn't selfish but necessary. Taking care of themselves had to be the top priority. By doing this, so many caregivers were personally revitalized and most claim that this change actually helped them become better caregivers!

Back to GRGs. At that moment, I realized the same concept applied here. Rather than focusing on the child in a GRG situation, we needed to be focusing more on the grandparent! I immediately called many of the GRGs on my list to confirm this belief. Not a single grandparent I talked with disagreed. For many, it was an epiphany. This was so exciting! The key ingredient we had all been searching for wasn't legislative or programmatic—it was a mindset! Romans 12:2 states a principle that may also be applied here, "Don't copy the behavior of this world, but let God transform you into a new person by changing the way you think" (NLT).

Be Yourself

As validated by what Norma said above, becoming a GRG (grandparent raising a grandchild) can call for serious adjustments: financial, time, emotional, physical, psychological. It doesn't have to turn your world upside down. You are perfectly fine the way you are. Keep operating as you have been operating. Focus on your own needs, desires, duties and ambitions, and create a plan that incorporates your own personal goals and needs as well as your grandchildren's.

GRGs I talk with, after broaching this subject, commonly tell me that they agree. Key advice they would give a new GRG is that there is incredible value in keeping your own life and your own plans on schedule. Those who radically altered everything in their lives typically regretted it. Successfully raising a grandchild means operating as normal but using your experience and intuition to guide you in what you need to do. If you are consistently engaged in prayer, God can use your intuition to help you make right decisions. Philippians 4:6 speaks to this principle, "Don't worry about anything, instead, pray about everything. Tell God what you need and thank him for all he has done" (NLT).

A Major Issue

Brooke and Kaitlyn are currently being raised by their grandparents. They are victims of an unfortunately common situation. Their mother, never married, became a drug addict and is now incarcerated. Thankfully, these young girls have caring grandparents who have taken them in and are providing a stable home environment.

According to the 2005 American Community Survey, there are more than four million children (one in 12) in this country being raised by grandparents. That's a startling number. From 1990 to 2000, the number of children being raised by their grandparents increased 30%. From all indications this trend will not only continue but will increase significantly over the next decade. Already some mental health professionals estimate that the number mentioned above has nearly doubled in the past eight years.

Many factors contribute to this phenomenon such as accidents, war, unwanted pregnancies, substance abuse, mental illness, divorce, and domestic violence. In Oklahoma, for example, nearly 60,000 (or 6.5%) children are being raised by their grandparents. This number continues to rise throughout the country.

Developing a Plan

Wilma loves her son dearly. At 19, John joined the Air Force and was stationed on the West Coast. While there, he married and the newlywed couple was soon expecting their first child. Wilma flew to the West Coast full of excitement, ready to become a first-time grandmother. During the delivery, however, complications arose. Although John welcomed into this world a beautiful son, the complications were severe and he lost his young wife. During the bittersweet struggle, Wilma realized that she would need to help John. They determined that he could not meet the rigorous demands of his job and appropriately raise the baby as a single father. It would be best if Wilma, at least temporarily, took the child.

I met Wilma at a conference in the spring of 2007, just after starting this chapter. As she related the story, tears in her eyes, we talked about how common this scenario is for GRGs. Not her specific case, but how so many of these situations develop rapidly and unexpectedly. Rarely are grandparents given much notice. The tendency is to panic. Although it is critical to determine what needs to happen immediately, it is even more important to take the time as soon as possible to develop a comprehensive, written plan. Wilma agreed. When we met that spring, she had been caring for that grandson a short three months. We sat down at a table and started putting together her plan. I couldn't help but think about what God said in the Bible: "For I know the plans I have for you. They are plans for good and not for disaster, to give you a future and a hope" Jeremiah 29:11 (TLT).

Fully assess the situation. Norma's situation is certainly unique. Regardless, when a GRG situation develops, it is imperative that you take the time to understand all of the circumstances. Buy a notebook and start keeping a journal. Begin crafting a plan. To start, ask yourself questions such as:

- *How did the situation develop?* Capture facts and opinions here. If some things could have been addressed earlier on to prevent this situation, how do you keep it from happening again down the road, maybe with a different adult child of yours?

- *Why was I selected to be the care provider?* Your answer can affirm your role and strengthen your resolve. In many caregiving cases, the most capable individual steps up and becomes the primary care provider. However, in other cases, individuals are sought out because of their strong faith rather than their capability.

- *How long will I be caring for this child?* Be realistic. Most GRG situations last far longer than expected. I suggest, as I did with Wilma, that you sketch out a scenario where you are the primary provider until the child reaches 18. It may help you to be less concerned about the future if there is at least one other person who can be trusted to care for the grandchild if you are no longer able to continue. Make sure that your desire is known to the one you expect to follow you. And be sure he or she is aware of and meets the state requirements to be a care provider for your grandchild if the need should arise.

- *What hurdles might I face?* Think through and attempt to resolve legal issues, health issues, dealing with the school system, families, finances, and the like on your own. Reach out to knowledgeable people such as pastors, social workers, and counselors who can help you deal with these challenges.

Learn what it takes in today's society. Second parenthood, or "reparenting," can be daunting. For many grandparents raising grandchildren, their last experience as parents came several decades ago. Boy, have times changed! One spry lady I met last year was raising a great-grandchild. This child was eight, entering the second grade. She was nearly 80. That generational gap was like the Grand Canyon! But I was delighted to find out that she was already on top of things. She had been to the child's elementary school, talked with the principal and teacher, signed up to be part of the PTA, and was immersing herself into the school system. Although that only represents one component of raising an eight-year-old, my guess was that she was well on her way to covering the other bases too. Although these are good resources, consult scripture passages such as: Proverbs 16:31; Deuteronomy 11:18; 1 John 3:11-24; 1 Timothy 4:1-5.

Find out what it takes to successfully raise a child today. Build relationships with other parents and grandparents who are rearing their children or grandchildren. Ask lots of questions. Watch select TV shows (maybe Oprah?), read pertinent magazines and books, check out websites. Just like you were preparing for a test, prepare for what's ahead. Don't blindly stumble along. Begin addressing questions like:

- How is raising a child different today than when I was last a parent?

- What are societal snares I need to be aware of? For those raising older grandchildren, be sure to monitor what they are doing on the Internet and who they are text messaging.

- What resources do I need? There are several great, affordable parenting magazines that can be very helpful.

Being smart about this will elevate your comfort level and hopefully prevent problems down the road. Most grandchildren admit they really suffer no ill effects (i.e., peer pressure or teasing from other kids) from being raised by their grandparents. So, tackle the issue with gusto and educate yourself!

Adjust as needed. Now that you have evaluated your situation, you are in a better position to understand what it takes to be a parent in today's times. You are ready to start making your first educated adjustments. Remember that you don't need to change everything in your life. That should not be necessary. However, it is likely you will need to make some adjustments.

- Am I equipped to fully meet this child's needs? Yes, you are. But, this question will help you recognize areas that you may need to adjust.

- Do I need to make some adjustments? These adjustments (i.e., time, money, social activities), if made early, can soften the burden.

- What impact will these adjustments have on me? An apparently selfish but very necessary question. You need to recognize the impact so you can plan accordingly. If being a GRG means trimming your fitness schedule, find other creative ways to stay physically active. Just trim and adjust, don't eliminate!

Okay, you've tackled a chunk of the task by developing a plan. The next segment, as we've discussed repeatedly, is vital. Norma told us this at the beginning of the chapter and countless other GRGs would shout the importance of this from the rafters: Take care of yourself!

Self-care is an area most often neglected. When these unexpected situations develop, your own needs begin to slide down the scale of importance. Before long, you are tired, stressed, unhappy, grouchy and depressed. This can happen in the blink of an eye. One day you feel you are in control. The next you feel like you are just holding on for dear life. Understandably, this will affect how well you parent.

Don't let this happen to you! Right up front, at the beginning of the GRG experience, make a promise to yourself that you'll take care of you! Keep that a top priority.

Support groups are important. Support groups are made up of people who are raising their grandchildren who get together regularly to share their experiences and make suggestions to each other about how they deal with the challenges mentioned above. These groups are misunderstood by many. Some think support groups are counseling sessions, with lots of crying and hugging and feel-good talk. In reality, most of the GRG support group meetings I have attended have been more like a well run corporate executive meeting. They start on time and end on time. The GRGs quickly bring the group up to speed on their situation, ask direct questions to see if others have ideas to help resolve a challenge they are facing, sharing facts and telling about recently discovered resources. Now, on occasion you'll see some crying and hugging, which is absolutely fine, but for the most part these meetings are a superb source of information.

- Is there a support group near you? Check churches and civic clubs. Some universities and non-profits host meetings as well.

- If not, should I start one? It's not difficult—we promise! There are suggestions on the Internet and most libraries have books that give easy instructions.

- What about online group options or other creative alternatives? Again, engaging in a support group can have lots of benefits. If your schedule won't allow it or geography prevents it, check online. Your grandchildren can probably tell you how to find a "chat group."

Hold on to what's important to you. Remember Norma's comments at the beginning of the chapter? She talked about how important it should have been to first meet her own needs. In doing that, rather than putting every ounce of energy and attention into her GRG situation, things "would have turned out differently." Since much of the chapter is devoted to this issue, we'll move on. Just make sure your mindset is where it needs to be!

Determine where you need help. Set your pride aside for a moment. Think very reasonably about this step. You don't have to—or need to—do it all. Asking for help is a major step in securing time and energy for you. Be careful about getting caught up with doing so many things that you ignore the relationship with you grandchildren. Pastor Charles Swindoll, commenting on Psalm 78:1-4, remarks that grandparents' favorite gesture is open arms. Grandparents don't look for mistakes, they forgive them. "Best of all," he says, "when you want to talk, they want to listen…They are there, even if not much is happening, they are there."

Earl was a burly, boisterous man who always wore overalls. When I first met Earl, he had been taking care of his daughter's son for the last several years (his daughter was 12 years old when she became pregnant). He arrived on that particular day for a GRG support group meeting seemingly confident and somewhat reluctant to be there, as though he was wasting his time. During much of the meeting, Earl said nothing. Finally, toward the end, a fellow GRG attendee said something that hit a nerve with Earl. She commented about how thankful she was for her sisters who would stop by to help with the granddaughter. Earl bristled. Then he went on a ten minute rampage about how lucky she was and how some people (namely Earl) have nobody to turn to for help—and he started crying! My guess is you could count on one hand the number of times Earl has cried in his life. Earl and I spent quite a bit of time together over the course of the next few days. We wrote down areas where he could use help and begin identifying family members and friends who might be willing to help. Sure enough, when we approached them they were more than happy to help! Earl had just never asked and since his demeanor was less than welcoming, few approached him. At the next meeting Earl was a different guy. He became one of our most outspoken advocates on the importance of taking time off from parenting (respite) and seeking help from others.

- *What responsibilities can I carry out myself and where could I use some help?* Think comprehensively about what must be done and in some cases you might find you can fully meet these responsibilities. In most cases, however, you'll find components where help may be needed and much appreciated. For Earl, one of the items was having someone who could assist his grandson with homework. As it turned out, Earl's church secretary was a retired teacher and was thrilled to give periodic tutoring. You will find, I promise, that having help with some of the smallest tasks can provide a huge benefit.

- *Who do I have that can help me?* Many of your friends and family members, as Earl finally realized, are happy to contribute if only asked. It brings joy into all of our lives to help a child.

Respite (rest, relaxation) is crucial. Respite is simply a "break," a chance to recharge your batteries. I have yet to talk with a caregiver or GRG who disagrees that respite is crucial. But, so few actually do it! Many consider this a low priority or don't see any feasible way to fit respite into their schedule or budget. Research strongly demonstrates how effective respite can be—it prevents burnout, helps maintain your well being, and enables you to be the best parent possible.

- *What type of respite is most valuable to me?* For some, it's golfing or some recreational activity. For many others it is even simpler… catching your favorite TV show, reading a book, taking a walk, working in the garden, watching a sunset, soaking in a hot bath or surfing the Internet.

- *How do I ensure that it remains a vital part of my schedule?* That can be the difficult part. Be sure, at all costs, that you keep this activity in your schedule. That is a critical piece to winning the self care game.

Now you have built a plan that includes all the important components of being a great parent again. Included in that is the ever-important focus on yourself. But—you are not done yet! The final task involves thinking about the big picture.

See the Bigger Picture

Identify ways to advocate. The experiences you and millions of others are going through are valuable lessons that need to be shared. You will find it incredibly refreshing when others appreciate your advice. In a strangely affirming way, advocating also reminds you that you are not alone. Many others are in the same boat, and the boat is larger than we ever thought it would be.

- *Do I know other GRGs?* Get to know them, seek their counsel and share your experiences. As we talked about earlier, they are everywhere. You will find them in the grocery stores, PTAs, churches, Sunday schools, community centers, or they may be your neighbors.

- *What can I do in my local community to help GRGs?* Maybe you need to start a support group. Pair up your skills with an identified need. Locally, we had an individual who felt it was important for each child in a GRG situation to begin the school year with a new pair of shoes. Her efforts started years ago and now it has grown into a huge program, fitting thousands of youngsters with new shoes each fall. If you are comfortable with this, take your efforts to the next level and begin working with your state legislature to develop programs and policies that help GRGs.

Visualize the outcome. I strongly believe in visualizing how you want the situation to turn out. This helps you see the forest instead of just focusing on the trees. Visualize this child grown, excelling in their chosen profession, bringing up children of their own in a stable home environment. It will put a big smile on your face. Then, graciously acknowledge the fact that *YOU* will have played a big role in making that a reality!

Embrace the opportunity. One of my favorite Bible verses is Jeremiah 29:11. I quoted it earlier. This opportunity has been given to you by God, but during the hard moments it isn't easy to accept as a blessing. Romans 8:28 promises, "We know that all things work together for good to them that love God…" If you are rearing your grandchild, you have been called. Rest assured, many will benefit from your example. You will grow, the child you are raising will be eternally thankful, and others will watch you and learn from the example you are setting.

Reread Barbara's quote at the beginning of this chapter. Relish each moment with enthused optimism. Embracing the opportunity will bring many unexpected blessings.

You are doing a marvelous job. Most of you reading this chapter would not know that I was actually raised by my grandparents. Consequently, this issue is dear to my heart and I find myself constantly advocating for GRGs. Let me briefly tell you my story. It is my prayer that the suggestions offered in this chapter will encourage and bless you in one of the most important roles a grandparent may be called on to play.

My mother and father were very young when I was born. Both were still in high school. Although they were not incapable, it was determined that the most stable environment for me would be with my mom's parents. Over the years, my grandpa ("papa") and grandma ("GG") showered me with love and affection. They instilled in me strong values, taught me to work hard, study hard and to be thankful. I didn't feel any differently than the other kids being raised by their traditional parents. My grandparents were involved in everything I did—school, athletics, etc. Now, reflecting back as an adult, I know it wasn't always as easy as it appeared. I know they sacrificed. Money was limited, time was precious. But, they juggled it well and always kept their cool. Although they never formally developed a plan to my knowledge, they saw the big picture. They knew it was important to press on with their own desires and ambitions, keep their marriage strong, and do the best they could do with me.

I might be biased, but I think I turned out alright! They raised a dedicated, passionate young man who works daily to improve the lives of older adults.

I tell you my story to reinforce this—things will be okay. I see so many grandparents fret and worry about how those grandchildren will turn out. You cannot control everything. Your job, quite simply, is to first take care of yourself and to secondly love that kid to pieces. You will do a marvelous job! Someday soon, like me, that grandchild will grow up and do well in life—and I promise they will credit you for their success!

Helpful Resources

I have found these websites to be beneficial in my work with grandparents raising grandchildren. Much of the information is free.

I encourage you to check them out and share them with others.

- AARP Grandparent Information Center: www.aarp.org/families/grandparents/
- Children's Defense Fund: www.childrensdefense.org
- GrandsPlace: www.grandsplace.com
- KINship Information Network: www.kinsupport.org
- National Aging Information Center: www.aoa.dhhs.gov
- The Grandparent Foundation: www.grandparenting.org
- Generations United: www.gu.org
- Piecing Hearts Together Again: www.raisingyourgrandchildren.com
- USA.Gov: www.usa.gov/Topics/Grandparents.shtml

Exercise

The authors thought it would be helpful to end the chapter with an exercise. I agree! Now, some of you reading this book may not be a GRG. It is likely, however, that you know a GRG. Look around—your workplace, civic club, church, fitness facility and neighborhood are likely places to find GRGs. Kindly encourage them. You may want to share this book with them.

For those GRGs reading this book, not surprisingly, I would urge you to go back through the chapter and review the suggestions. By the time you are done, you will have developed a great document. This document will increase your comfort level as a GRG. It will further encourage you in your role and ensure that you keep the right mindset. Take care of yourself!

Prayer

Dear Lord, thank you for the privilege of raising my grandchildren. Give me the strength and wisdom needed to bring them up to follow in the footsteps of your words. Help my grandchildren to see what is good in your sight and live according to your commandments. Watch over us and protect us in these days of uncertainty. May our lives be acceptable to thee and honor you each day with the lives we live. Amen.

chapter 6

ETHNICITY AS A RESOURCE IN GRANDPARENTING

SO GOD CREATED PEOPLE IN HIS OWN IMAGE. GOD PATTERNED THEM AFTER HIMSELF, MALE AND FEMALE HE CREATED THEM.
GENESIS 1:27 NLT

BUT RUTH REPLIED, "DON'T URGE ME TO LEAVE YOU OR TO TURN BACK FROM YOU. WHERE YOU GO I WILL GO, AND WHERE YOU STAY I WILL STAY. YOUR PEOPLE WILL BE MY PEOPLE AND YOUR GOD MY GOD…"
RUTH 1:16 NIV

> WE ALL KNOW GRANDPARENTS WHOSE VALUES TRANSCEND PASSING FADS AND PRESSURES, AND WHO POSSESS THE WISDOM OF DISTILLED PAIN AND JOY. BECAUSE THEY ARE USUALLY FREE TO LOVE AND GUIDE AND BEFRIEND THE YOUNG WITHOUT PRIDE AND FEAR OF FAILURE AND CLOSE THE SPACE BETWEEN GENERATIONS.
> PRESIDENT JIMMY CARTER, SEPTEMBER 9, 1979, PROCLAMATION OF NATIONAL GRANDPARENTS' DAY

Satchel Paige, the renowned African American baseball pitcher, called one of his pitches a "bee ball." He was often asked why he named that pitch a bee ball. Paige responded with a huge grin, saying, "I call it a bee ball because when it crosses the plate it will *be* where I want it to be." Many ethnic grandparents have dedicated much of their lives to guiding their grandchildren in such a way that they will cross home plate having accomplished all God created them to *be*. Although they may not always have the resources to help their grandchildren achieve, a majority of ethnic grandparents will sacrifice everything they have to help them to *be*come all they can be. Several studies by family specialists have found that ethnic mothers and grandmothers have an intense desire to see their children advance in society.

In the Bible, Ruth and Naomi illustrate one of the best examples of the blending of ethnic backgrounds and their story illustrates the importance of grandparenting. Ruth, a Moabitess, married Boaz, a Jew who became Naomi's "kinsman-redeemer" in order to provide Naomi's dead son with an heir. Although there was no blood relationship, the child was recognized by Jewish society as Naomi's grandson. That grandson was King David's grandfather and an ancestor of Jesus (Ruth 4:13-17). Too often in our society, ethnicity is viewed as a problem rather than a resource. We want to draw your attention to the value of your ethnicity as a resource in grandparenting. Celebrating ethnicity brings history, culture, socialization, and relationships into the lives of children and grandchildren that would otherwise be lost. Proverbs 14:26 underscores the key characteristic that will make this quality a powerful reality, "Those who fear the Lord are secure; he will be a place of refuge for their children" (NLT).

A major strength of American society is its diversity. From the beginning, America has been blessed with people groups from all parts of the world, desiring to be free to pursue opportunities for themselves and their families. Throughout history ethnic minority groups have made and continue to make numerous contributions to the American way of life. Early in our history, society was divided, informally, into what is termed "majority" groups and "minority" groups. These terms refer primarily to political and economic power positions. The majority group is the one whose will dominates society. The minority group does not have the political and economic voice to impose its will on society as a whole. Some use the term "racial group" as a synonym for "ethnicity." The term ethnicity, however, comes from the Greek word *ethnos*, which simply means *peoples*. Thus, all identified groups are ethnic groups. This includes European Americans, African Americans, Hispanic Americans, Asian Americans, and Native Americans.

Unfortunately, this fact is often overlooked due to a considerable amount of racism in our country. Although progress has been made in living up to the Constitution and Bill of Rights regarding equality, there is still considerable injustice. In a small way we believe that this chapter will counteract racism by focusing on groups of grandparents who are known for their strength and commitment as a result of their ethnicity. Grandparents, regardless of their ethnic affiliation, can provide the path away from segregation and discrimination.

Whenever the word ethnicity is used, it is important to move beyond the physical characteristics such as color of skin or shape of the face. In this chapter we use the term ethnicity to draw attention to the uniqueness of each ethnic group discussed, regardless of physical characteristics. Hopefully, what you read will affect your grandparenting career in a positive way.

Regardless of which ethnic group is discussed in this chapter, most grandparents hope that their grandchildren will have opportunities to experience "life, liberty and the pursuit of happiness." However, words such as racism, segregation, prejudice, and abuse have described their experiences most of their lives.

Ethnic grandparents see themselves as responsible for continuing the traditions and values of their particular group. This also serves to uphold the freedom promised in the United States Constitution. They wish to prepare their grandchildren for life and do everything possible to minimize the inequality they have experienced. They are building solid foundations on love, sacrifice, and readiness to do whatever is necessary for their grandchildren. A significant number of the U.S. military come from all the ethnic groups.

We will look at six different ethnic groups and the way their grandparenting careers are implemented. Each ethnic minority group is unique and special in the way it approaches teaching its beliefs and values. The six groups selected include Hispanic Americans, African Americans, Jewish Americans, Native Americans, Asian Americans, and European Americans. We could not cover every possible ethnic group in this chapter so we chose to highlight several that are representative of the total grandparenting population.

Historically, all people groups in America came from another part of the world. They brought with them family traditions, values, and practices. As these groups settled into their new environments, their traditions may have changed. The generations that came after them often found that their traditions and values had to be adjusted if they were to be accepted in the established culture. Thus it became the primary responsibility of grandparents to instruct the grandchildren in the ways of their ethnic traditions. They were the keepers of the family histories and values. They take seriously Proverbs 13:22, which states that "Good people leave an inheritance to their grandchildren..." (KJV). While most want to leave a material inheritance, the greatest will be the values and heritage grandparents leave to their grandchildren.

Charles Handy, in his book *The Age of Paradox*, speaks of the tendency to skip a generation—that is, instead of children listening to parents, they cross over and pay more attention to grandparents.[11] This insight is found to be true in the case of ethnic multigenerational families. Ethnic minority grandparents appear to have a better grasp of their culture than their adult children. This situation is prevalent in the United States due to adopting a significant

---

11 Charles Handy, *The Age of Paradox* (Boston: The Harvard Business School Press, 1994).

amount of prevailing American culture. Pastoral psychologist Walter Houston Clark, after studying second and third generation Irish immigrants to America, observed, "What the son wishes to forget, the grandson wishes to remember."[12]

A famous Dallas Cowboy linebacker, Dat Nguyen, an immigrant from Viet Nam, quickly adopted the American way of life. He attended Texas A&M University and succeeded not only in academics but also in playing football. He says that his success was largely due to the values of the Viet Nam people. His grandparents and parents instilled in him the importance of never giving up. They taught him to never be a slacker in his work. He learned that regardless of the hardships, there is always a way to succeed.[13]

One of the common characteristics of most ethnic minority grandparents is that they have a basic love of life. Little things do mean a lot. Their roots reach deep into their ancestry and provide an anchorage that gives them a clear image of who they are and provides a sense of pride and esteem. These attitudes are often observed by grandchildren and used as a foundation upon which they build their lives.

Native Americans

Native American grandparenting styles have been identified as: Cultural conservator, custodian, ceremonial, distanced, and surrogate.[14] When grandparents are not available to pass on the values,

---

12   John W. Drakeford, *Psychology In Search of a Soul* (Nashville: Broadman Press, 1964).
13   Nguyen, Dat, *Dat: Tackling Life and the NFL* (College Station, Texas: Texas A & M University Press, 2005).
14   Joan Weibel-Orlando, "Grandparenting Styles: Native American Perspectives," in Alexis Walker, Margaret Manoogian-O'Dell, Lori A McGraw and Diana White, eds., *Families in Later Life* (Thousand Oaks, CA: Pine Forge Press, 2001), 135-144.

the grandchildren are deprived. For example, a Native American drug and alcohol counselor remarked, "Since most of our young families live in the cities, their children do not spend much time with their grandparents. There seems to be little respect for authority, the law, or for life that was normally taught to children by their grandparents." This is due to changes in the lives of Native American tribes where nearly 80% of young adults and their families live in the cities while the older adults remain on the reservations. In the past, grandparents were very important in the values formation of their grandchildren. They did this by telling stories that contained examples of Native American traditions. Such stories were very entertaining and instilled the traditional values of the people.

Today's Native American parents are generally busy working outside the home. Their children watch television rather than listen to their grandparents tell the traditional stories. Native American leaders are concerned, justifiably so, because for a culture to survive, traditions must be transmitted from one generation to another. That has been, for most ethnic groups, the primary role of grandparents.[15] Native American groups today are probably doing as much as any ethnic minority to compensate for the difficulties caused by shifts in the culture.

In the motion picture *Flags of Our Fathers,* a young Marine who helped raise the flag on Iwo Jima during World War II was a Navajo. He experienced major value conflicts because he was required to act in a way that was contrary to the values he learned from his family on the reservation. In the motion picture *Code Talkers,* Americans observed how valuable ethnic minority contributions can be to this country. As depicted in the movie, aging Native Americans are

---

15   Donald E. Gelfand, *Aging and Ethnicity* (New York: Springer Publishing Company, 1994), 24.

regarded as elders, people of substance and value, by their tribes and families—but this can sometimes be disrupted by separation and distance.

The story is told of an older Native American woman that illustrates this point. She wanted to return home to her tribe after being separated for years from her roots. She had left the reservation to live and work in Los Angeles. Her culture required her to reenter her tribal community and search for her rightful role in it. This process turned out to be longer and more complicated than she anticipated. Tribal leaders finally give her a new identity based on her potential as a surrogate grandparent. She applied for authorization to become a surrogate grandparent at the tribal social services agency and received approval to become a foster grandparent, raising as many as four grandchildren. These children include both foster and biological grandchildren. In this case, reidentifying with her tribe and receiving positive acceptance demonstrates the importance of ethnicity.[16]

Jewish Americans

Jewish Americans have the longest history of any known recorded ethnic group. The scriptures, beginning in Genesis, tell their story including promises, trials, and victories as a people. One of the most famous people in Jewish history was Abraham who is called the father of the nations.[17] Abraham's legacy is shared from generation to generation through traditional ceremonies and the teachings of grandparents to grandchildren.

---

16   Joan Weibel-Orlando, "You Can Go Home Again," in Elizabeth W. Markson and Lisa Ann Hollis-Sawyer, eds. *Intersections of Aging: Readings in Social Gerontology* (Los Angeles, CA: Roxbury Publishing Co., 2000) 157-166.
17   Genesis Chapters 12-25.

In Judaism, as in other ethnic minorities, grandparents are held in high esteem. Elders receive much respect by being ensured a prominent position in the family for as long they live. Jewish grandparents are often identified by such names as "Bubby" (from Russian "Babushka) for the grandmother (Hebrew-Savta) and "Saba" for the grandfather. Another custom that recognizes the importance of grandparents to families is when their children's children are named after them, following their death.

Important events for Jewish grandparents have to do with the high holidays in the fall of the year: Rosh Hashanah and Yom Kippur. Hanukkah and Passover, though not high holy days, are significant festivals as well. During these special days, Jewish families reaffirm their Judaism and the importance of every member of the family. Jewish grandmothers sing important prayers to their grandchildren, usually sung in Yiddish and interpreted to their children.

When someone dies there is a ritual called "shiva." Shiva is a name for Judiasm's week-long period of grief and mourning for the seven first-degree relatives (mother-father, husband-wife, sister-brother, children, and perhaps grandparents). For eleven months, a prayer—kaddish—is said every day, usually by the eldest son of the deceased. This important time gives emphasis to the connection between generations. Grandparents are often consulted about some of the rituals associated with this time that may have been forgotten. "Tallit," usually the first prayer shawl owned by the grandchildren (typically purchased for the boy or girl by the grandparents), is given to them at their Bar Mitzvah or Bat Mitzvah.

Since nearly half of their grandchildren are not being raised "Jewishly," Jewish American grandparents consider this loss of tradition to be a primary concern. This signals a major shift in the spiritual makeup of American Jewish families.[18] Oral history, such as stories about the Holocaust or visits to Israel, is an effective way to keep grandchildren aware of their heritage. Another way is for grandparents to recite the family genealogy and quiz the grandchildren. Jewish culture is rich in history and tradition. To provide you with a more complete picture of this ethnic grandparenting career would take another chapter or two. The point to remember about this ethnic group is that every aspect of their lives has some ritual or ceremony that gives grandparents possibly more opportunities than any other ethnic group to ensure that Jewishness continues in their grandchildren and great-grandchildren. Psalm 128:6 emphasizes this promise, "Yea, thou shalt see thy children's children, and peace upon Israel" (KJV).

Hispanic Americans

Hispanics Americans are drawing considerable attention these days because they now constitute the largest minority group in America. Recent discussions about the increase in Hispanic immigration (both legal and illegal) by population experts have made them more visible. Part of this discussion is that Hispanic families tend to have higher birthrates than other ethnic minorities. In addition, more young Hispanics than ever are going to college and moving up in American society.

To understand grandparenting in the Hispanic culture, we need to look at the various generations. Hispanic grandparents who have been lifelong citizens of the United States will have very different experiences than those who are first, second, or third generation

---

18   Yosef Abramowitz, "Grandparents can boost Jewish Identity," in *Jewish News of Greater Phoenix*, http://www.jewishaz.com/jewishnews/971128/yosi.shtml, downloaded 5/29/2007.

immigrants. Immigrants face completely different obstacles to blending into society, finding work and becoming citizens. Each generation can expect things to be different than the one before.

Another group with a different take on grandparenting is those who continue to live in their homeland while trying to have a relationship with their grandchildren from a distance. Their homelands include many countries. When grandparents of the earlier generations have part of their identity in their country of birth and the other part in the United States, it is difficult for them to carry out the grandparent careers according to cultural traditions. Barriers to satisfying relationships between Hispanic grandparents and grandchildren may include language and distance as a result of increased mobility of families, and technology.

When you look at all of these generational and geographic situations, the Hispanic ethnic group is, in reality, many sub-ethnic groups. The thing that connects them is their language and their relationship, historically, to Spain. As a result, many expressions of grandparenting careers may exist among the various Hispanic sub-ethnic groups. Understanding where they have come from helps us to understand some of the behaviors of the Hispanic group. For instance, Hispanics take great risks in coming to the United States. They do this so they can provide a better life for all their family members, including grandparents. The Mexican American celebration of Cinco de Mayo is evidence of the importance of freedom to this group of people.

It is also helpful to understand some of the Hispanic names used within the family. Like most ethnic groups, Hispanics have several names that distinguish grandparents and great-grandparents. A great-grandfather might be called "Papa Grande," a great-grandmother

"Mama Grande," a grandfather "Abuelo" or affectionately "Abuelito," and a grandmother "Abuela" or affectionately "Abuelita." Other names are "Modrina" for godmother and "Padrino" for godfather. The quality spoken of in Proverbs 15:4, "Gentle words bring life and health…" appears to be the dominant characteristic remembered by Hispanic grandchildren.

As with other ethnic groups, religion plays a significant role. Traditionally, Hispanic people have been identified with the Roman Catholic Church. More recently, although a majority remains Catholic, greater numbers of Hispanic people in North, Central, and South America have become involved in other churches and religious organizations. This religious diversity is also influencing family structures and family traditions, including grandparenting careers.

Several influences in the Hispanic population have affected waves of grandparents' immigration to the United States. In some generations, "barrios"—or concentrated Hispanic neighborhoods—were formed, giving more opportunity for the Hispanic culture to be passed on by the grandparents. But later generations were more involved with the assimilation process than remembering their heritage, thus learning English and attending public schools where a secular education was emphasized, and leaving another gap between grandparents, their adult children and their grandchildren. Mixed marriages added another complication to the kinship structure and the resulting dilution of the heritage being passed down.

Undergirding all of these influences was the limited financial resources of the Hispanic family. Nationally, Hispanic household wealth equals less than 10% of the wealth of European American households. Grandparents are needed more than ever to provide the identity, support, and stability in their families. For example, the teenage pregnancy rate of Hispanic granddaughters is over 20%. In most cities, Hispanic youth gangs function as a surrogate family to many Hispanic teens and preteens. The absence of resident grandparents may explain the prevalence of such gang activity. A solution to this problem is multifaceted, but one part would be the restabilization of the Hispanic home where grandparents are intimately involved with their grandchildren. History has demonstrated that where this condition exists, children appear to grow up with much stronger traditional values. In Hispanic families in America where grandparents live with or near their adult children and grandchildren, there is a greater possibility that higher moral values will prevail.

Asian Americans

Older members of some Asian societies are thought of in two ways: 1) *vertical society*—a delicately graded hierarchy with chronological age more important than other characteristics; and 2) *filial piety* based on the tradition of respect and duty toward parents and grandparents that has its roots in ancestor worship.[19] Ancestral worship exemplifies the place of religion in honoring older family members, which is shared by many ethnic groups. Asian grandparents do not necessarily live with their adult children and grandchildren because of necessity, but because their culture has prepared them for this living relationship. For an Asian family to ignore that tradition would be a violation of their moral and religious heritage.

One of the authors was privileged to spend a year at the Center for the Study of East-West Relations in Hawaii, studying the aging populations of a variety of cultures. Here he learned about traditional practices in Asian cultures as well as cultural shifts brought on

---

19 Jill Quadagno, *Aging and the Life Course* (Boston: McGraw Hill, 2002), 33.

by more countries being added to the growing list of aging nations. Traditionally, Asian grandparents are expected to live with their adult children and grandchildren. Grandparents hold positions of honor and esteem in Asian American families. This position affords them a powerful platform from which to teach their grandchildren regarding cultural, national, and family history. Asian adult children expect their aging parents to live with them and help with the household chores, including the caring and rearing of the children.

Asian cultures are historically "collectivistic." That is, individuals are expected to contribute to the family's collective well-being rather than pursue success for themselves alone. If they succeed they enhance the family's reputation. If they fail, the whole family fails. The family honor is at stake; therefore, Asian American students are recognized for a strong work and study ethic. Grandparents enable this process by instilling in the grandchildren the importance of their family heritage and family honor, and by holding the grandchildren accountable.

African Americans

African American grandparents, especially grandmothers, hold a powerful place in the family. African American grandparents are, according to a number of writers, given an active role in parenting. They are generally endowed with the same authority as parents. One African American grandson said, "Mother Wilson, my grandmother, lived next door. I would spend about as much time at her house as in my mother's. When I misbehaved, she would spank me with a paddle she kept hanging on her kitchen wall. Neither my mother nor I ever thought there was anything unusual about that. It is what grandmothers do. I knew that she would give her life for me and my seven brothers and sisters. We respected her authority as much as we did our mother's."

Some social historians trace the strong role of women in the African American population to the practice of plantation slave owners. Often the woman with children would be separated from the children's father. The total family responsibility fell on the women of the family, including grandmothers, to rear the children. It became the primary responsibility of grandmothers to pass on the heritage to the whole family. Singing was a major vehicle for transmitting a significant part of their cultural heritage. African Americans, as with grandparents of other ethnic groups, passed down much of their cultural history through story telling. Some of the story telling was specifically oral history. Other story telling was for the passing on of family traditions and values.

European American

Survival is the theme of many of the stories grandparents tell their children in every ethnic group, including the majority ethnic group, European Americans. Although there continues to be considerable focus on individuality and success among European Americans, it appears that family is becoming more important to the Boomer population (includes members from all ethnic groups). There appears to be more diversity among European American majority grandparents than ethnic minority grandparenting careers. European American grandparents also appear more ethnocentric—that is, they rely more heavily on their position for identity than their traditional ethnic backgrounds. As a result, within the European American ethnic group, you find greater variation in their identity and grandparenting career paths. Although love is apparent in each group, there are wide differences in how love is expressed for grandchildren. Love usually takes the form of materialism such as gifts, bank accounts, travel, and financing college education. Other expressions of love are similar to those of other ethnic grandparents.

European Americans tend to be fascinated with genealogies and some are looking to grandparents and great-grandparents for specific information regarding their ethnic-cultural history. At one time in the last century, few European Americans would admit they were related to other racial groups. After the Second World War in the middle of the 20th century, there seemed to be a resurgence of interest in ethnic heritage. At the end of the 20th century and the beginning of the 21st century, for example, many European Americans are proudly claiming their relationship to Native American tribes. Some are openly discussing the fact that they may be related by blood to African ancestors. Most easily discuss their relationship with the Caucasian peoples of Western Europe. Often, however, grandparents have lost their own connections with their cultural histories.

Older people, including grandparents, are repositories of traditions and values. Some of these values come from their religion and spiritual traditions. Other values come from a family heritage that has been passed down from generation to generation. The means by which these values were transmitted came primarily through the relationship between grandparents and grandchildren. We do not mean to imply that all of the values passed to grandchildren by grandparents are desirable. Racism, for example, is one of the undesirable attitudes that some grandparents have taught their grandchildren. Forms of racism are practiced by people in power positions in every sector of the United States. Many older people have learned to live with the contradictions in what their religion teaches about such issues as racism, homosexuality, cohabitation without marriage, abortion, euthanasia, and other ethical issues, and what they actually practice. Grandparents would do well to remember that they are teaching their grandchildren by what they say as well as what they do.

Mixed Ethnic Identity

One situation arising in this diverse society is how to deal with people who come from families of two or more ethnic groups. The problem comes to the surface in most educational settings when children and grandchildren are forced to choose one ethnic group over another in identifying who they are when applying for admission to college or applying for a job. The implications of this forced choice have significant consequences for grandparents. How do the grandparents of an ethnic group not selected as part of their grandchildren's identity deal with this decision? Does this mean that the grandparents of the ethnic group selected as the grandchildren's choice of identity have more privileges than the grandparents not chosen? Is there a way that both sets of grandparents can equally be recognized as the grandchild's family in choosing his or her identity? These questions have yet to be answered by the major institutions in American society.

In summary, whether it is fully recognized or not, ethnicity impacts all grandparents. Whether your grandchild's ethnicity is emphasized or despised, it will still affect the grandchild in ways that perhaps were not intended. Or in ways that celebrate the uniqueness and value of the distinctiveness of our country's immigrants.

Dr. Ruth Westheimer, often associated with sex education, is also known as a proud grandmother. Dr. Westheimer, in her book

Grandparenthood, says it best in describing the importance of grandparenting in upholding traditions. She says that traditions not only involve preservation and adoption, but it also includes invention.[20] In other words, grandparents link the past, the present and the future together to enlarge the traditions of every ethnic group.

As you select the grandparenting career that best fits you, it is beneficial to consider the answers you would give to the following questions. Begin by inventorying your history and ethnic traditions. Once you complete the inventory, ask yourself:

- How do my history and traditions define my grandparenting career?
- How will the above answer influence the integration of the old with the new culture?
- Where do I place the grandparenting career with other careers that make up my lifestyle?
- Will some of my careers need to shift priorities due to the increasing demands of the expanding career of grandparenting?
- How is my faith tradition influencing the way I grandparent?
- How much do I rely on my holy book for direction and guidance in relating to my grandchildren?
- When conflict enters (and it will) into my career as a grandparent, how will I handle it when everyone disagrees on values?

---

20 Ruth K. Westheimer and Steven Kaplan, *Grandparenthood* (New York: Rutledge, 1998), 26.

- In my grandparenting career, what will my adult children and grandchildren remember as part of my legacy?

Although this assignment may be difficult and uncomfortable, it will give you food for thought and help you in designing a grandparenting career that is consistent with who you are.

Prayer

Our God, thank you for our ethnic heritage. You have blessed us with a culture that is strong and confident. May we recognize you as our God, the creator of the universe, the ever-present, the all-knowing, all-powerful God that we can know regardless of our ethnicity. Help us as grandparents to share our faith with our grandchildren and direct us in helping them see that our faith is far more than our culture. Thank you for all that you continue to do for our families and especially our grandchildren. Amen.

chapter 7

GRANDPARENTS ACHIEVING SPIRITUAL WELL-BEING

> SINCE YOU HAVE BEEN RAISED WITH CHRIST SET YOUR HEARTS ON THINGS ABOVE WHERE CHRIST IS SEATED AT THE RIGHT HAND OF GOD. SET YOUR MINDS ON THINGS ABOVE, NOT ON EARTHLY THINGS.
> COLOSSIANS 3:1-2

> LET THE CHAIN OF SECOND CAUSES BE EVER SO LONG, THE FIRST LINK IS ALWAYS IN GOD'S HAND.
> LAVINGTON

Many people seem to fear computers. You've heard people say, "I don't like to work with anything that is smarter than me." In fact, computers are not exceptionally smart. They only know one way to do anything, i.e., the way their programmer designed them. Without a human programmer and operator the computer can do nothing. The same case could be made for human beings trying to operate without God. Irene Endicott agrees with the importance we place on the role of spirituality in grandparenting in her book *Grandparenting Redefined*. In her opening chapter she gives a job description for grandparenting in which she says the place of employment is anywhere, the hours of employment are at any time, the qualifications are the love of Jesus Christ, the patience of Job, the wisdom of Solomon, the grace of God, the forgiveness of the Holy Spirit, the perseverance of Paul and a sense of humor.[21] In our rapidly changing world it is important to hold on to "something" that is constant, consistent, and comprehensive.

It's in these times of rapid change that we often seek a "compass" for helping us navigate our life journey. We may start to discover that the "isms" in our lives, such as materialism, judgmentalism, legalism, hedonism, and intellectualism, have not given us the fullness and satisfaction we expected from life. It is times like these when we need to take a second look at spirituality and religion as possible answers to our search for a more complete and meaningful life. Spirituality and religion are not synonymous terms. Religion, for most people, is a process that enables spiritual formation. On the other hand, we are spiritual in the same way we are physical, social, mental, and emotional. We may or may not be religious, but we are spiritual beings.

Spirituality refers to the essence of life. Indicators of our spirituality may be seen in our lifestyles. People experiencing a healthy and growing spirituality have a positive appreciation of life. They may experience a declining and debilitating spirituality if their view of life is negative and depressive. Author Rick Warren talks about a healthy spirituality connected with a "purpose driven life" and

---

[21] Irene M. Endicott, *Grandparenting Redefined: Guidance for Today's Changing Family* (Lynnwood, WA: Aglow Publications, 1992), 19.

provides a blueprint for a lifestyle based on God's eternal purposes rather than cultural values.[22] Many years ago an Englishman, J. B. Phillips, saw this situation with great clarity. He said, "The trouble with many people today is that they have not found a God big enough for modern needs."[23] Phillips observed that the spiritual dilemma many face has to do with a misunderstanding of the true nature of God and God's capacity to be concerned with every aspect of people's lives. Dallas Willard speaks of a paradox in the contemporary experience and understanding of "hearing God." On the one hand, "We have a massive testimony to and widespread faith in God's personal, guiding communication…on the other hand we also find a pervasive and often painful uncertainty about how hearing God's voice actually works today…"[24] Keith Miller writes an entire chapter titled "Communicating a living faith to one's own children—an unchartered sea." Miller's insights can easily be applied to grandparents. Perhaps we are "putting the cart before the horse." Instead of beginning with sharing our spiritual life with our grandchildren, it might be wise to assess our own spiritual well-being.[25]

Dan Sutherland states that "as long as we are content with the status quo, we will not discover God's vision."[26] Yet there is something wonderful awaiting us, as God reveals in scripture: "God has a plan for you, a plan of hope and meaning" (Jeremiah 29:11). As a grandparent with a reservoir of family wisdom, it becomes even more important to understand God's will for your life and the mission of sharing faith with your grandchildren rather than simply a religion.

---

22   Rick Warren, *Purpose Driven Life* (Grand Rapids: Zondervan, 2002), flap.
23   J. B. Phillips, *Your God Is Too Small* (New York: The Macmillan Company, 1955), v.
24   Dallas Willard, *Hearing God* (Downers Grove, IL: InterVarsity Press, 1999), 25.
25   Keith Miller, *A Second Touch* (Waco, TX: Word Books, 1967), 37 ff.
26   Dan Sutherland, *Transitioning* (Grand Rapids: Zondervan, 2000), 29.

Most likely you want your grandchildren to experience the love, grace, and freedom that is ideally promised in the Judeo-Christian faith. So much religion is culturally based, but spirituality is boundless. Faith is not culturally bound or limited to one expression.

Molly Srode, author of *Creating a Spiritual Retirement* and co-publisher of the "Senior Spirituality Newsletter," suggests that exploration of the human spirit means letting go of who we *were* and finding out who we really *are*. Much of our identity is based on the past and may not be pertinent to contemporary life. Faith transcends time and it is more than theology. Strode writes, "Now is the time to perceive our spiritual dimension—the strong, silent, presence of our spirit."[27] Strode assumes that all of us are created in the image of God (Genesis). In other words, our true selves can only be discovered through acknowledging the wholeness of our individuality. That is, along with our acceptance of the physical, mental, and emotional dimension of life, there is a spiritual dimension requiring the same amount of attention. To pursue this realm, it is important to define some terms such as spirituality, spiritual well-being, and spiritual growth. As we explore and discover our spirituality, you will see how the process begins to help you in your relationships with your grandchildren. The apostle Paul says that "…the fruit of the spirit is love, joy, peace, patience, kindness, goodness, faithfulness, gentleness, and self control …" (Galatians 5:22-23). Would you agree that these attributes are ideal qualities of a graceful grandparent?

Perhaps one of the best descriptions of what grandparents need to be when they are at their best is found in the definition of

---

[27] Mary Srode, *Creating a Spiritual Retirement* (Woodstock, Vermont: Skylight Paths Publishing, 2003), 29-33.

"spiritual well-being" offered by the National Interfaith Coalition on Aging: "Spiritual well-being is the affirmation of life in a relationship with God, self, others, and the environment that nurtures and celebrates wholeness."[28] Derrel, one of the authors, helped to develop this definition when he was working as a researcher for the National Interfaith Coalition on Aging in the early 1970s.

Affirmation of Life

Every generation engages in a never ending struggle with the meaning of life. It is hardly easy for anyone. It can be especially difficult for people who have reared their children and retired from employment to then try to make sense out of the days, weeks, months and years that seem to pass by so rapidly.[29] Younger grandparents may find their lives so filled with activity that they feel they can hardly breathe. This is complicated by the number of "isms" 21st century grandparents encounter in their everyday lives. This situation for grandparents can be resolved positively by recognizing the fact that, with God's help, life can be full and meaningful. Successful grandparents are the ones who find that with each challenge, God provides the emotional, physical, and spiritual resources to accomplish whatever situation they face. Over the years we have interviewed several hundred grandparents. Most have testified to their belief in the validity of the Bible. We believe that "All scripture is God breathed and is useful for teaching, rebuking, correcting and training in righteousness" as found in 2 Timothy 3:16 (NIV). Perhaps the Phillips translation is easier to understand and

---

28 James A Thorson and Thomas C. Cook, Jr., *Spiritual Well-Being of the Elderly* (Springfield, IL: Charles C. Thomas, 1980).
29 George Barna, *Revolution* (Carol Stream, IL:Tyndale, 2005), 47.

apply to grandparenting: "All scripture is inspired by God and is useful for teaching the faith and correcting error, for resetting the direction of people's lives and training them in good living."

Relationship with God

Grandparenting works more effectively when we understand that there is a Divine Being who has created both males and females in his image. Likewise, this Divine Being reminds us that "he knows our name" (Psalm 103). We are tightly linked with our Creator; God is always with us.

It may be difficult for grandparents to realize that God loves them even more than they love their grandchildren. God demonstrates all the types of love expressed in the ancient Greek language: agape, phileo, storge, and eros. God's love for grandparents is probably best expressed by "agape." Agape is an all inclusive type of love that is intentional, involves choice, and includes affection (eros), friendliness (phileo), and storge (parent's love for a child). There are times when we are filled with elation and joy. At other times we feel the presence of One who is closer than a brother or sister. Then there are times when we know that our Holy Parent is there to comfort and guide us even when we can't feel his presence.

For you as a grandparent to experience the full meaning of a relationship with God, it is important to learn who God is, and that he desires a closer, more intimate relationship with you. Accepting God's love for you and returning that love will result in a growing faith and a sense of spiritual wellness.

Faith is more than doctrine and works; it is assurance of God's love and presence. The scriptures state that "without faith it is impossible to please God" (Hebrews 11:6). God does not expect you to be perfect or to perform superhuman deeds. You express your love for God through faithfully pursuing your grandparenting path. You can rest assured that you will never be alone because God will always be with you (Matthew 28:20; Psalm 23).

Relationship with Family and Friends

All humanity has been created for relationships with each other and with God. The Creator never intended that we would achieve our purpose on earth as "Lone Rangers." Although the male was created first, the account in the book of Genesis emphasizes that humanity was created male and female because it was not good for humans to be alone (Genesis 1:27; 2:18). Human history is essentially about relationships of one kind or another. Most of the biblical narratives are about relationships between God and humanity, and about human relationships with each other. The Ten Commandments reflect this in very specific ways. When Jesus was asked about the first or greatest commandment, his response underscores the importance of relationships to our spiritual well-being. He quoted from Deuteronomy and Leviticus, "Love the Lord you God with all your soul and with all your mind. This is the first and greatest commandment. And the second is like it: Love your neighbor as yourself. All the Law and the Prophets hang on these two commandments" (Matthew 22:37-40, NIV).

What this means to grandparenting is that more attention should be given to the nonmaterial aspects of relationships. There should be greater emphasis on understanding and accepting, rather than rejecting grandchildren whose lifestyles are different ... focusing on long-lasting involvement, assuring grandchildren that you are there to walk with them regardless of the circumstances.

Relationship with Self

It is easy to understand how Fred, a 71-year-old, might think that he is not worth anything to anybody, given the fact that he is no longer employed, and has arthritis, diabetes and hypertension. At the community senior citizen center he is often heard saying, "We ought to be ashamed of ourselves. We aren't worth a dime and all we are doing is taking up space." He doesn't appear to be depressed, but he doesn't seem to enjoy his life either. He says the only joy he gets out of life is visiting with his grandchildren about once each month.

Harold, who is 82 years old, has a totally different attitude toward life. He volunteers to help "widow women" on his street by mowing their lawns and doing minor repairs on their houses. He drives forty miles each weekend to visit with his daughter and her three children. He says he believes that every day is sacred to God and it is his responsibility to make the most of it. He likes to quote from Genesis 1 and 2, where the Bible says we are created in God's image and given a purpose. He says that when his purpose here on earth is over, he believes God will call him home. Harold likes to quote a sign he saw at his church, "I know I am important because God didn't make no junk! I am just one of God's antiques and that makes me more valuable every year."

Glenda, a 37-year-old single grandmother, first felt that her world had come to an end when her 17-year-old daughter Cindy returned home from college in the middle of the semester. Cindy was pregnant and her boyfriend wanted nothing to do with marriage and fatherhood. Glenda felt that somehow she was to blame for her daughter's situation and began to experience deep depression.

Glenda sought help from a number of sources, but nothing seemed to help until a counselor at her church said to her, "Think about it a moment. Why are you feeling so guilty? Did you instruct Cindy to get pregnant or was her pregnancy the result of her own decisions and behaviors? Do you love her less because she messed up? Do you think you will not love your grandchild because she did not come into this world the way you wanted?"

Glenda said, "Of course not! I still love Cindy and I am going to love my grandbaby."

The counselor said, "Can you forgive yourself for what you think was your failure in raising Cindy?"

Glenda responded, "I see what you mean. I don't know what I could have done to prevent this. She is really a good girl. Right now she needs me to be there for her. With God's help, we are going to get through this."

Most of today's grandparents were very likely raised with the teaching that we should love God first, others second and self last. Some Christians have suggested that we reverse this by saying it is important to love self first so we can love others and to love others before we can love God. They are basing this reverse thought on their belief that it may be impossible to love God without loving self and others first. This notion is a result of thinking that everything has to happen in sequence, one after another. Relationships with God, self, and others don't always happen the way we expect and they aren't always easy to explain. We love ourselves, and at the same time we love God, and at the same time we love our children and grandchildren and friends. When Jesus said that we love God and neighbor as self, he was not giving a rank order or sequence, but explaining that these objects are all to be loved at the same time. If one love object is out of the loop, the whole relationship system becomes "out of whack."

Relationship with the Environment

Grandparenting careers are lived out in both a physical and a social environment. Your house or apartment, located in a neighborhood, town or city, constitutes a significant portion of the physical environment. A few years ago we participated in a "life satisfaction survey" to discover how satisfied grandparents were with where they were living. Researchers guessed that people would always be satisfied if they could continue living in their own homes; a little less satisfied in a retirement village; even less satisfied in an extended health care facility, etc.

What we found was that there were people who were not satisfied in each of those living arrangements, and at the same time there were people who were very happy in each of those environments. We discovered that the attitude and behavior of the people played a major role in determining who was happy with their living arrangements and who was not. If people felt they had a choice, they felt better about their environment. If they chose to make the most of their circumstances rather than complaining about them, they were more likely to be satisfied with their housing. One woman told of her mother's positive approach. When they were in the lobby of the nursing home, her mother spoke up and said, "I am going to love my room and I am going to like my roommate. These people are wonderful and I am going to enjoy being here." The daughter said, "Mother, you haven't even seen your room yet and you haven't met any of these people. How do you know you're going to enjoy being here?" Her mother said, "When I was praying this morning it came to me that it was my choice. If I chose to like my room and the people, it was going to be alright."

The survey also showed that most grandparents would prefer

to live near their grandchildren and be with them as they grow up. Sometimes, however, this is impossible because of distance and other circumstances. The chapter in this book on distance grandparenting may provide some useful suggestions for dealing with this type of environmental stress.

Some grandparents live in the same house with their adult children and grandchildren. Often this can be workable and pleasant, but at other times it may be a source of conflict. Sarah, in her late 50s, lives with her daughter, son-in-law, and two teenage grandchildren. Her husband died suddenly a couple of years ago with a heart attack. He did not have insurance and they had only a meager savings account. She had to get along with her Social Security income. Sarah and her adult children decided that they needed to sell the family home to pay off outstanding debts. They decided that Sarah would move in with her daughter who could provide her a room of her own. At first it seemed to be a very good arrangement, but the situation soon disintegrated. Use of the kitchen was the first point of contention. Sarah wanted to rearrange the kitchen utensils and appliances. Then she and her daughter argued over how the teenage grandchildren were disciplined. Fortunately, they made an appointment with a gerocounselor who was able to help the family work through their differences and settle into a relatively peaceful living relationship.

As social and physical environments change, it is important that we be prepared to change with them. Grandparents who intentionally try to understand their grandchildren's culture are discovering that their relationships are better and their opinions are more appreciated.

Two major factors for dealing with the tensions and stresses of living with your children and grandchildren are your capacity to deal with stress, and the level of the stress itself. The key to success is ensuring that the stress does not exceed your capacity to deal with it. As a grandparent, you can do this by honestly assessing your capacity in terms of energy, time, money, and patience with your unique family situation. For example, if you plan for a special time with your grandchildren and the weather prohibits outdoor activities, then you need to be able to adjust your expectations and transfer outdoor activities indoors in a way that allows for everyone to have an enjoyable time with as little stress as possible.

Nurturing and Celebrating Wholeness

Relationships with your loved ones are dynamic and therefore need continual care. You want to be the best you can be—spiritually, mentally, and physically—to give your relationships the care they deserve. Above all, your spiritual wellness will help you in every aspect of your life as you continue to adapt to changes and grow in your relationship with God. This should be an intentional process rather than simply saying to yourself, "Whatever will be will be" and waiting for something to happen.

To help you move forward in your spiritual journey, take a passage of scripture such as Psalm 23, and let it be your guide for this next phase of your life. Take note that this Psalm is more about life than death. True it is often used in situations where someone is dead or is dying. But in your journey, think more of what Psalm 23 says about life. Just as the shepherd watches over and cares for every need of the sheep, God is watching over and providing for your every need as a grandparent. When life circumstances seem to be more than we can bear, God walks with us through the valleys and continues to provide what we need to sustain us. The Psalm also tells us that even when our lives are threatened, we will be able to feel God's presence with us, and when the end of this life comes, we will be seated in the eternal presence of God. His constancy and promises leave nothing to fear.

Grandparenting is a complex career that requires more than the thoughts of human beings. Proverbs 16:9 says, "In his heart a man plans his course, but the Lord determines his steps." He truly knows the big picture and can guide us in ways we can never understand. We encourage you to seek his counsel—study the scriptures, pray often, and rely upon you faith, being open, and sensitive to hearing his voice. The apostle Peter makes it very clear that we can cast all our anxiety on him because he cares for us (1 Peter 5:7).

Become more aware of the importance of your spiritual health. Give it as much attention as you do your physical and mental health. Someone is always encouraging us to have an annual health checkup. In the same way, give yourself an annual "faith checkup." Spend some private time with God. It will strengthen your faith and clarify his purpose for you as a grandparent. Remind yourself that God desires to help you and cares about each detail of your life. Spend time each day reading God's Word. The psalmist says, "Your word is a lamp unto my feet and a light for my path" (Psalm 119:105, NIV). And Ralph Waldo Emerson says, "Do not go where the path may lead, but go instead where there is no path and leave a trail." Your grandchildren are noticing the spiritual trails you are leaving. You can celebrate the fact that no matter what condition your body is in or under what conditions you are living, when you intentionally focus on positive relationships with those you love and with your God, life will be filled with a sense of wholeness and joy.

Prayer

Dear Lord, I desire to grow in my relationship with you. Guide me as I search the scriptures to learn more about the love you have for me and my grandchildren. May your leadership keep me focused on those things that will last for eternity. Prepare me to share my faith with each grandchild so they may have the peace and joy only you can give. Make me a blessing for those who are also seeking to be godly grandparents. Amen.

chapter 8

GRANDPARENTS AND THEIR ADULT CHILDREN

CHILDREN, OBEY YOUR PARENTS IN THE LORD FOR THIS IS RIGHT. HONOR YOUR FATHER AND MOTHER...
    EPHESIANS 6:1 NIV

AND NOW A WORD TO YOU PARENTS. DON'T MAKE YOUR CHILDREN ANGRY BY THE WAY YOU TREAT THEM. RATHER, BRING THEM UP WITH THE DISCIPLINE AND INSTRUCTION APPROVED BY THE LORD.
    EPHESIANS 6:4 NLT

IT SEEMS TO ME THAT PERSONS WHO HAVE THE MOST SUCCESS ARE THOSE WHO SOMEHOW TURN SELF-CARING INTO WHAT MIGHT BE CALLED OTHER-CARING.
    ARTHUR GORDON

Martha, a 79-year-old grandmother, asked the conference leader, "What do you do when you and your daughter don't agree about how to discipline the children? I don't believe 12-year-old girls should be dating boys at all. My daughter thinks I am stuck in another generation and out of touch with what is acceptable for young girls." Before the conference leader could respond another woman asked, "Are you living at your daughter's house?"

Martha said, "Yes."

"Then bite your tongue," the other woman advised.

Martha responded, "My tongue already feels like hamburger meat." There were more than fifty older people in the room. Most of them were nodding their heads in understanding.

"I don't know what all the fuss is about," said Carl, a large slightly bald man of 76 years. "My children and grandchildren are constantly trying to get me to come and live with them. I don't recall ever having an argument with any of them. I simply welcome them when they come to visit and try to get by their houses when I can. Someday I may need to move in with one of them, but right now it is not an issue."

It may be strange at first to talk about parents and their adult children in a book about grandparenting. After thinking about it you will agree that relationships between parent and adult child impact others in the multigenerational family. Possibly the relationship most affected is the parent's relationship with their son or daughter's children (your grandchildren). The purpose of this chapter is to take a closer look at one of the most important and enduring relations found in the family. Our approach will be to look at relationships from the parent's perspective and then look at the relationship from the perspective of the adult children. Next, a number of circumstances, both good and bad, that might be a consequence affecting the relationships grandparents desire with their grandchildren. We'll briefly identify and discuss some of the most common issues in the adult-parent/adult-child relationship. And at the end of the chapter we'll provide suggestions that may help maintain and improve relationships between grandparents and their adult children.

Caring, Bonding and Boundaries

If there is one word that summarizes the parent and adult child's relationship it would be *caring*. From the beginning most parents do the best they can to love, protect, and encourage their offspring each day of their lives. Their efforts and expectations do not abruptly come to a halt once their children become adults. If anything, the desire to love, encourage and protect intensifies as the years go by. There is, however, one difference. Although this relationship will continue for the rest of life, there is a major shift from being a parent to building a friendship rather than an authority-child relationship. In the past your children may have cautiously avoided your best advice, but now they must make their own choices and move forward in the way they think is best. Parents of adult children begin to sense that their major contribution to their children is to be a good host and listener. "When they do things differently than you would do them you learn to keep your mouth shut," as one wise parent put it. Of course, this is not totally true, but you can see how it could happen from time to time.

We have noted, from our experience, that parents often have a number of expectations for what their adult children will do for them when they need help. Most often, these are not written down anywhere. Quite often these parents are not disappointed. There are, however, many occasions when we have counseled with older families about the parent's complaint that they cannot count on their children.

Adult children, who are grateful for everything their parents did for them, will come to the aid of their parents when there is a need. They feel that their parents did what they did unconditionally. Ideally, in all the ways the parents helped, there were no strings attached. When strings have been attached, however, adult children often feel "put upon."

Adult children do not necessarily want to follow in their parents' footsteps. Research shows that one generation skips another in its search for direction and guidance. What this means is that adult children may reach out to their grandparents for advice rather than their parents. The reason for this leap may be that parents sometimes live vicariously through their adult children while their grandparents provide the freedom children seek as they create their own pathways. While adult children may overlook their parents' advice, it is still common for them to express love toward their parents in ways that are not immediately visible. A bond usually exists between parents and children that seems to be greater than any explanation known to the experts. We believe it is a spiritual connection. It is a type of love that is expressed by the ancient Greek word *storge* that describes the love of both parents and adult children for one another. It is similar to God's love for each of us, which is expressed by the word *agape* that is most often used to express this godly love. An example is stated in Romans 5:5, "For we know how dearly God loves us, because he has given us the Holy Spirit to fill our hearts with his love" (NLT). Agape is the ancient Greek word used in this passage. God has given it to us as a model. It includes the type of love we are to have for each other in the family and in the larger "family of God." It is best described in 1 Corinthians 13. We believe that if this type of love is practiced by everyone in each of the generations in families, they would experience a piece of heaven on earth.

One of the best ways to express that two people are bonded is to say that they "matter" to each other.[30] When we speak of mattering to others and others to us, we mean accepting each other completely, as we are, and rejecting any attitude or behavior that causes anyone in the relationship to feel like a non-person. Solomon, in Ecclesiastes 4:10, reminds us of the value of bonding when he says, "Woe to the one who falls when there is not another to lift him up." For example, have you ever felt like a third wheel where two people are already involved in a conversation? You try to become a part of the conversation. As you make a comment there is a moment of silence. The two people look at one another and then continue to converse as though you were not there. You have been defined by their actions as a non-person. Being treated as a non-person feels worse than being rejected.

As a general rule, parents give sacrificially to their children. Their identity as mother and dad often takes priority over their husband and wife roles. This happens in all the different types of families mentioned in this book. This, of course, impacts grandparenting.

How does *mattering* show itself in the grandparent-adult child relationship? One example is listening to one another without interrupting before the story is complete. A negative example is where the conversation is one sided and someone does not feel they are heard. A number of adult children share their frustration of being

---

30   Dave Carder, Earl Henslin, John Townsend, Henry Cloud, and Alice Braw, *Secrets of your Family Tree* (Chicago: Moody Press, 1991), 148.

on the telephone with their parents who do not respect their opinions. Or, the grandparent is frustrated when they try to talk with their adult child and feel that their opinions and desires are ignored. These grandparents often feel left out, although they will readily say that they know they do matter to their adult children.

It's difficult to separate caring from bonding. Think of your relationship with your adult child as different sides of the same coin. You cannot know that you and your child feel close (bonded) to each other unless there is also a sense of caring for each other.

A factor that is often overlooked and not associated with caring and bonding is boundaries. Even though caring and bonding suggest freedom to be oneself in the family, the established boundaries often interfere with meaningful relationships. Caring and bonding suggest attachment while boundaries suggest separation. All of us at one time or another, whether it be in family, church, or business, have said, "I need my space." Boundaries do not necessarily communicate a lack of desire or need to be with loved ones. Rather, it is a time when we seek rest, introspection, and possibly "time out." Time out does not just apply to disciplining children as we often hear the term used. Adults, both parents and adult children, need time to be still and experience quietness, relaxation, and to be free from a schedule. This is necessary for personal renewal, which makes caring and bonding possible. When boundaries are missing in family relationships the result is "enmeshment" where people are not free to be themselves. The absence of boundaries contributes to stress in relationships.

Stressors in Grandparent-Adult Child Relationships

Family history has sometimes been likened to an explorer negotiating a forest without a map. So much of what families experience seems to be unexpected. Both successes and failures are common. And, they don't necessarily look like hills and valleys—they may be more like interstate highway lanes running parallel with each other.

Embarrassing mistakes can almost be guaranteed. These are referred to as the "family secrets" and they are not to be shared outside family boundaries. One of the stressors surfaces when a grandparent shares a family secret with the grandchild about something the adult child did as a youth. While this may be amusing to share, it can also create friction. For example, a grandfather loved to tell tales about some of the mischievous pranks his son, their father, played on his brothers and sisters when they were growing up. When the grandchild copied one of the pranks and caused some discomfort to one of his sisters, he was disciplined by his father. The grandson became very angry and challenged his father. "Granddaddy told us you did the same thing once." To which the father could only reply, "Yes, but it was wrong for me to do it then and it is wrong for you to do it now." The adult son later confronted his father and asked him to not tell any more stories of that nature to the children.

At other times you may create stress by telling secrets that undermine the parents' attempt to motivate the grandchild and to be positive role models—for example, sharing information about the parents' grades that were not very good or how they were sent to the principal's office for some irresponsible behavior. Stories like these are best left to the parents to share with their children.

Comparing your grandchildren's success with their parents' accomplishments can be damaging as well. Your grandchildren may not have the same type of intelligence, talents, interests, or other gifts as their parents. If you emphasize the accomplishments of your adult children to your grandchildren, you could cause your grandchildren to feel inadequate. You should nurture and encourage your grandchildren's natural talents and interests without expectations that they follow the same path as the parents. This will help them grow into strong, confident adults.

Involving your grandchildren in some activity without their parents' permission can cause stress in your relationship with your adult children. Grandparents sometimes feel they don't need to get permission to take their grandchildren on a trip, for example, or to buy them special toys. You should always be respectful of the parents' authority and ask for permission. The same goes for financial matters. It is always best to ask the parents first if you wish to give or loan money to the grandchildren to avoid a potentially stressful situation.

When grandchildren see their parents talking back to you, it can suggest that the grandchildren have permission to treat you the same way, and eventually their behavior toward their parents, too, will mirror that poor behavior. Children are adept at imitating what they see the most important people in their lives doing. Take, for example, Mr. Alton. He moved in with his son and family. Mr. Alton had a debilitating disease that so embarrassed his son that he and the daughter-in-law built a small house in the back yard where they would take Mr. Alton food away from the family. He would wear a plastic bib and eat at a table by himself. One day, the son saw the grandson building a toy house. He asked him what he was doing. The grandson answered, "I am building a house for you to live in when you come to live with me."

Gift giving can be another stressor. Some adult children object to their parents bringing the grandchildren gifts every time they come to visit. They want the grandchildren to look forward to seeing the grandparents rather than expecting a gift every time. Try to be sensitive to the parents' wishes and ask beforehand if a gift is okay.

Oftentimes parents will experience pressure within their church to bring up their children in that particular faith. This can happen in any denomination or any religious group. For example, Sam and Carolyn met, fell in love, and were married. Sam was Protestant and Carolyn was Catholic. When the first grandchild was born, both sets of grandparents insisted that the child be brought up in their church. This situation calls for some judicious decision making. An experienced and wise third party (such as a professional counselor) may be helpful.

Spoken words can also be a point of contention. Sometimes adult children express their independence by using language that may be abrasive or derogatory. Along with language, manners can be a stress area, too. The adult children may not realize or seem to care that what they are doing has an adverse effect on the grandchildren. For example, it is the custom in many families to not begin a meal until everyone is seated. If in the adult child's home that custom is not practiced, the grandchildren may not understand what is expected at the grandparent's home. When the "rules" are not clear, it becomes difficult to understand what is expected. It is important that you, as a grandparent, model the appropriate behavior even if your children do not appear to remember what you taught them. Being a good role model is probably the only thing that can help. Lecturing, most often, will only bring a negative retort and create family conflict.

Demonstration of affection can also be a point of stress for the grandchild and possibly the grandparent. Sometimes the manner in which affection is expressed can be uncomfortable to grandchildren and the adult children are forced to make choices that may create a problem in their relationship with relatives. Sometimes grandchildren are "ordered" to respond to a grandparent with a kiss on the cheek. The grandmother, in turn, kisses the grandchild and leaves a considerable amount of lipstick on the child's cheek. Needless to say, the grandchild begins to wipe off the kiss in front of everybody, making the situation uncomfortable for all involved. Children, at different stages in life, have different attitudes toward open expressions of affection. Vinny, for example, when he was younger, loved to greet his grandmother and grandfather with a hug. It didn't matter to him then who was around. His grandparents looked forward to getting hugs from Vinny. After Vinny turned thirteen, however, he suddenly became distant to his grandparents' show of affection in public. In private when no one else was around, he would readily embrace either of his grandparents. The grandparents wisely respected this change in his public behavior because they understood that his resistance was not about his love for them. When he was eighteen and in college, he became the same affectionate boy he had been in his preteen years.

One final example of a stress inducer is when grandparents focus total attention on living only for their grandchildren. This can cause their adult children to feel excluded. The adult children and others may feel that there is something peculiar or wrong about this obsession.

The above-mentioned stressors are only samples. There are many more. Most of the time they can be managed by using basic common sense and seeking advice from wise family members. If, however, these and other stressors become disruptive and unmanageable, it is advisable to seek help outside such as a pastor, social worker, or professional counselor.

Identifying or Expressing Feelings

Some families experience situations where strong feelings are generated. The ideal response when this happens would be if all the parties were open and talked through things and were able to resolve their differences. Often, however, we "bottle up" our feelings and do not express them. They are then allowed to fester, which leads to emotional strain in relationships between grandparents and their adult children. When you and your adult children have expectations that are not met, there's a tendency to feel anger or rejection. If these feelings are expressed in a healthy way, however, they can be resolved and often lead to even closer relationships. If they are not resolved they can lead to a disruption in relationships—sometimes lasting months or even years.

Scripting

There is a belief in society that there is only one way to grandparent and a "script" for the way adult children should behave in relation to their parents. The script outlines both do's and don'ts. They represent what society thinks we *should* do rather than what we *want* to do. The accepted script gives very little attention to feelings, beliefs, or values that an individual grandparent considers important. To continue the theatrical metaphor, the script directs when one is to be "on stage" and when to be "off stage." Scripting leaves very little room for grandparents to express their individuality.

Unfortunately this script most often given to grandparents comes by way of their adult children. For example, the grandparent might want to watch his grandchild learn to swim. The parents of the grandchild give a birthday party where the grandson gets his first swimming lesson. The grandfather is not invited, but his son's friends are. The son defined the situation according to an accepted script—"grandparents don't need to be involved with this activity"—without considering the grandfather's or the grandchildren's feelings. Sometimes adult siblings informally discuss the script and team up to impose it on the grandparents. Or, family members may join together to impose a script on the adult children.

Trianglization

Parent-child-grandchild relationships sometimes demonstrate what family counselors refer to as "trianglization." This situation arises when one of the parties in the triangle attempts to manipulate another. For example, if adult children want to force a grandparent to make a decision in their favor, they might restrict access to the grandchildren. They know that the grandparent loves the grandchildren and will do almost anything to maintain a relationship with them. Another example: It is not unusual for grandparents to use their support for the grandchildren to persuade the adult children to comply with one or more of their wishes. Grandchildren are not above using their grandparents to get their parents to give them something they want.

Suggestions

It may appear from what you have read thus far that there are more challenges than blessings in the relationship between grandparents and their adult children. Nothing could be further from the truth. All families, at one time or another, will be faced with some of the circumstances discussed in this chapter. However, experience shows that you can be successful dealing with these challenges and maximizing growth opportunities within your family by becoming knowledgeable and aware, and getting the appropriate support when needed. To assist you in your relationship with your adult children, we offer the following suggestions. They are not exhaustive or failproof but your simply taking the time to be aware of them will go a long way toward improving your family relationships. Your success will rely heavily on the values, caring, bonding, and boundaries that have been characteristic of your family as well as those that are in place at the present time. A word of caution: This relationship was much easier to deal with when there was only one set of parents for the children. When children choose a mate and marry, another set of parents enters the picture. This addition can be either a hindrance or a help in realizing your desire to be an effective grandparent.

Tips for Grandparents with Adult Children

- Be thankful and express gratitude often for your adult children and your grandchildren.

- Be good to yourself. It has often been said, "Don't 'should' on yourself." Grandparents sometimes unwisely assume full responsibility for any difficulties that arise. Take responsibility only for the things *you* have done and the decisions *you* have made. *Shoulds*, *oughts*, and *musts* can be problems if they are overdone. A wise minister once said, "God doesn't want you confessing sins you did not commit."

- Practice forgiveness. Often we remember those things that hurt or disappointed us without realizing the importance of cleaning the slate. Understand that all of us make mistakes and if we expect people to forgive us, we need also to forgive them. We will do well to forgive ourselves as well.

- Recognize that all of us are a work in progress. Change is certain. Acknowledge and understand as much as you can the changes that will occur in your adult children as they have their own families and conduct their own lives.

- Inventory your values, those things that are important to you. Let your behavior match the positive values that make you who you are. It is important to acknowledge that some values are not positive. If you find some of those among your values, try to minimize and eventually eliminate them.

- Be open to new traditions that may be established in your adult children's homes that will most certainly influence your grandchildren. Respect the changes and do your best to see the positive aspects in these new traditions.

We encourage you to make application of these suggestions when they may be helpful. At the same time, you can add new suggestions to the list that will even strengthen your bonding with your children and grandchildren.

Prayer

Dear Heavenly Father, when I think of how you gracefully relate to me, my children, and grandchildren, I want to be more like you in all my dealings with my family. Please, God, help me to be wise in the way I make decisions that affect my children as they try to raise my precious grandchildren. I pray that you will give them the wisdom to seek your pleasure in all the ways they respond to me as their parent. May what we as a family do always bring honor to your name. Amen.

chapter 9

GRANDPARENTING AND THE LAW

> MOSES CALLED ALL THE PEOPLE OF ISRAEL TOGETHER AND SAID, "LISTEN CAREFULLY TO ALL THE LAWS AND REGULATIONS I AM GIVING YOU TODAY. LEARN THEM AND BE SURE TO OBEY THEM...STAY ON THE PATH THAT THE LORD YOUR GOD HAS COMMANDED YOU TO FOLLOW. THEN YOU WILL LIVE LONG AND PROSPEROUS LIVES IN THE LAND...
> — DEUTERONOMY 5:1, 33 NLT

> KNOW WHERE TO FIND THE INFORMATION AND HOW TO USE IT—THAT'S THE SECRET OF SUCCESS.
> — ALBERT EINSTEIN

There is no sweeter relationship than that of grandparent and grandchild. Although at first it may seem strange to ponder the rights and responsibilities that arise from such a sacred bond, every grandparent should be generally familiar with a few legal aspects of grandparenting. The good news is you're halfway there; you have found the information and when you've read this chapter, you will know how to use it.

The laws that affect grandparenting arise from both state and federal sources. Laws may differ from state to state, but don't let this frighten you. In every state there are professionals trained to help you navigate these waters. Many of these professionals provide a free initial consultation, and many states have legal aid or senior law centers that provide legal services at reduced prices based on your income.

The goal of this chapter is to discuss some aspects of grandparenting that you might not have previously considered. This chapter does not include legal advice. If you identify legal issues that might affect you, or if you want to know more about your state's law, contact a lawyer or legal aid representative in your area. You might also check the Internet. Many states have created websites that summarize their laws affecting grandparents, and provide links and contact information for your area.

Many times grandparents seek legal advice regarding their rights and responsibilities when a grandchild is thinking about or has already come to live with them. Situations leading to a change in the living arrangement or caregiving responsibilities for a child involve more than just legal issues. They impact the child, the parents, the grandparents, and the family as a whole in very basic and yet very profound ways. Change is rarely easy. Feelings, fears, and hopes for the future don't change with the stroke of a pen or the entry of a court's order. The aftershock of these changes may be felt for generations to come.

During any time of change it is important to be alert to your emotional, spiritual, intellectual, and physical needs, and to those of the child and other "family" members, whether or not related by blood or marriage. Use the tools you have learned about in other parts of this book to maintain your balance so that your grandparenting experience will be a rich one even amid change.

Grandparenting: A Legal Relationship

Most common legal issues that involve grandparents relate to your relationship with your grandchildren, such as the right to see your grandchildren or to temporarily or permanently raise them. Generally, parents are responsible for the care and welfare of their children. However, every grandparent who has an "in person" relationship with a grandchild may at some time need the legal authority to make decisions on behalf of that child. For example, you may need to make medical decisions for a grandchild temporarily left in your care or to enroll your grandchild in school.

Some grandparents may want to explore their legal right to visit a grandchild when one or both of the child's parents have died, the parents have divorced, or unmarried parents end their relationship. Other grandparents, either willingly or unwillingly, have become their grandchild's primary caregiver because one or both of the child's parents have died, are incarcerated, or have abused or neglected the child.

In addition to legal issues relating to decision making, some grandparents are interested in creating an estate plan that will provide financial security for a grandchild, or tax-related legal planning to set aside funds for a grandchild's education. These legal issues are directly affected by your personal financial situation and are outside the scope of this chapter. You should recognize, however, that the law provides a number of ways for you to provide for the financial well-being of your grandchildren and a lawyer trained in these areas can help.

Know your Geek Squad

Just because you own a computer doesn't mean you know how to fix it. Grandparenting is no different. The legal aspect of grandparenting is not about what you know, but *who* you know. Every grandparent should keep a list of contact information for a few professionals who can answer questions and provide assistance when needed, including the following:

- Area aging agency
- Geriatric social worker
- Child welfare worker
- Lawyer/legal aid/senior law resource center
- Local youth services agency
- Local caregiver support agency

These professionals should be able to help you identify the issues that pertain to your specific situation and help connect you to area resources that address those issues. Don't give up. If you are searching for information or assistance, it sometimes takes patience and hard work, but most often you will be able to find someone who has encountered your situation before and can help.

Proof of Legal Guardianship

When you were a kid, if your grandparent wanted to take you to the doctor, enroll you in school, or get your report card, chances are that's just what they did—no strings attached. Well, times have changed. To log onto your computer, you input your username and password. To prove that you are authorized to receive information or make certain medical, financial, and educational decisions about your grandchild, you may need one of the legal documents described below.

The type of document you need generally depends on the type of information or authority you are seeking. If you need information about your grandchild but don't need authority to make decisions for the child, a Release of Information form signed by the child's parents will often suffice. This type of document is merely an agreement that permits a school, doctor or similar provider to share confidential information with you about your grandchild. It typically does not require any special wording or court approval.

Grandparents who need to make decisions regarding their grandchild's care in addition to merely receiving information may need a Power of Attorney. A Power of Attorney is a more formal agreement signed by the child's parents authorizing you to make the decisions or take the actions described in the document. A Power of Attorney is often used when grandparents will be caring for their grandchildren on a temporary basis—for example, when the child's parents are in the military or on a long vacation.

Your state's law will identify the components that create an enforceable Power of Attorney. Some states have Parental Powers of Attorney, Special or Limited Powers of Attorney, and General Powers of Attorney. Each of these types of documents is used for different purposes and is enforceable for different periods of time. Often, pre-printed Power of Attorney forms that comply with your state's law are available. If you use a preprinted form without consulting a lawyer, be sure it itemizes (or permits you to write in) the specific acts for which you seek authority and that it will be effective for the length of time you need.

Some states have adopted a medical consent form that permits an adult such as a grandparent to obtain medical services for the child and may be used in lieu of a full-blown Power of Attorney. Keep in mind that a medical consent form will only give you the authority to obtain medical services. As a practical matter it may not involve much more effort to obtain a Power of Attorney that will give you greater authority to act on behalf of your grandchild. As always, if you are unsure which type of document fits your needs best, consult a local lawyer.

Access

Another common legal issue affecting grandparents is the ability to visit their grandchild. Although every state has laws addressing grandparents' visitation rights, these laws are not the same from state to state. Generally, you may visit your grandchildren when they are with your child. If, however, your child does not have or does not exercise visitation rights, or does not permit you to visit the children, you may have to obtain a court order for visitation. The court may consider the best interests of the child when ruling on an application for visitation, but in the U.S. the right of a fit parent to make childrearing decisions (including decisions about who will visit the child) carries more weight. This means that even though your request for visitation may be reasonable, a court may deny or restrict your request if that's what the child's parents want.

When families are informal, blended, or non-traditional, obtaining visitation rights may be more complicated or uncertain. It is easiest and typically most desirable if the parents and grandparents of the child agree upon visitation and respect the terms of such agreements to avoid the need of court intervention. If an agreement can't be reached, you might want to ask a trusted friend or professional such as a clergy person, counselor or social worker to help mediate an agreement that is fair and reasonable for everyone. In any event, you should keep in mind the child's best interests and emotional welfare. Be mindful of approaching any such negotiations in a loving manner so that you may avoid injuring the very relationship you are so passionately trying to keep intact.

Sudden Grandparenting

When those new grandchildren arrive, you dream of watching them grow up and hope and pray that their parents will do a good job of raising them. Sometimes though, our dreams become nightmares. The unanticipated death or incarceration of a child's parents, the involuntary removal of a child from the parents' home, or similar events may lead a grandparent to become the child's primary caregiver. Now you are the one who must pray for God's wisdom to do a good job of raising your grandchildren. Fortunately God, in James 1:5, promises to provide that wisdom.

The 2000 U.S. Census estimates that more than 4.5 million children live with their grandparents, and that 2.4 million grandparents are living with and responsible for their grandchildren. From 1990 to 2000, the number of grandparents raising grandchildren increased by 30%. This trend is on the rise. Knowing your choices before such an event occurs can eliminate some of the stress and uncertainty during this time of transition.

Be prepared. One of the first steps you should take is to ask your children if they have executed a will or other legal document naming the persons they would like to have raise their children should they die. Although a court will ultimately decide who will raise the children in the event of both parents' death, the parents' written wishes will be carefully considered. In making custody decisions, the court will also consider the child's best interest. This may include balancing such factors as kinship, financial stability, location of the parties seeking custody, and the like. Advance planning will help ensure that the parents' wishes are honored and will minimize the financial and emotional cost of later custodial proceedings.

Informal custody. A grandparent who houses and cares for a grandchild with no legal arrangement in place has physical but not legal custody of the child. The parents will retain legal custody and the right to remove the child and make decisions regarding the child's care. Under this type of arrangement you generally will not qualify for financial assistance or receive government-funded services to help you raise the child. As discussed above, you also will not have the authority to make decisions about your grandchild or receive confidential information. Although this is the simplest form of custodial care, it is unpredictable and exposes the child to further changes during a time when the child may need a sense of security.

Foster grandparenting. Foster care is a system that provides for the temporary placement of a child who has been removed from its birth family because of abuse or neglect. A child who is in foster care remains in the state's legal custody. Many state laws favor "kinship" placement of a child in foster care, which provides medical and financial support to grandparents fostering their grandchildren. The risk of foster placement is that the state has the right to remove the child from your care under certain circumstances.

Foster grandparenting is often a wonderful way to care for your grandchildren while their parents make personal or environmental changes required to earn the return of their children. Many times you will have access to social workers, therapists, and other professionals who can provide support to you and your grandchildren during this period. State financial support is also available to foster grandparents, and some states continue to provide financial support to children who are initially fostered by their grandparents and later adopted.

Guardianship. Legal guardianship is granted by a court. To seek guardianship you must file a petition asking to remove some of the rights held by the child's parents. Guardianships are governed by state law and may be "full" or "limited." A limited guardianship may be initially suggested by a case worker when a child is removed from the parent's custody based on allegations of abuse or neglect. A guardian may not be entitled to receive financial assistance or services available to a child who is in foster care. In other words, if you serve as your grandchild's guardian instead of their foster grandparent, you may have to use your own money to support the child. If you are living on a fixed income, this may be an important factor to consider when you are deciding what rights to pursue.

You may seek a full guardianship if you are raising your grandchild but his or her parents have never agreed to give you any legal rights, or if they die, are missing, incarcerated, or determined to be mentally incompetent. A full guardianship may apply to the child's "person" and/or to the child's "property." If you are appointed a guardian, under state law you will probably be required to file regular reports showing the court that you are appropriately caring for the child and/or the child's property.

Guardianship carries certain legal powers and rights that are not associated with other arrangements such as foster care or Powers of Attorney. Although some states permit a grandparent to prepare and file guardianship papers and to appear in court "pro se" (which means "on your own behalf"), you should consult a lawyer so that you will understand the rights and responsibilities of the various types of guardianships under your state's law.

Legal custody. Legal custody is also court-ordered and is a relationship that falls somewhere between guardianship and adoption. As with guardianship, before removing legal custody from the parents, the court will consider the child's best interest. This decision is often not an easy one, and courts are generally reluctant to remove a child from the legal custody of his or her parents. Even though legal custody is more secure than informal custody, a custodianship does not legally end the parental relationship, and the court may later reverse the custodianship and return the child to his or her parents.

Adoption. Adoption is the most permanent change in the legal relationship between you and your grandchild. You may adopt your grandchild with the parents' consent, or without the parents' consent if a court has terminated their parental rights (which may occur in connection with abuse or neglect). An adoption is a legal proceeding that removes all of the parents' legal rights to have custody of the child, and transfers those legal rights to the grandparent.

Adoption is a permanent step and should be carefully considered before undertaken. Because of its permanency adoption may help a child feel safe and secure, but the adoption process can also cause stress and conflict that may leave the child feeling "caught in the middle." If you are considering adopting your grandchild, be sure that both you and the child have access to appropriate counseling and support services. Take the time to talk with the child and help him understand the process and meaning of an adoption, and to reassure him that he is loved and cared for. Remember that by adopting your grandchild you will be stepping into the role of parent. This transition may be difficult for you, your spouse, the child, and your other children and grandchildren.

Native American grandchildren. The rights and responsibilities of grandparents seeking custody or adoption of Native American children are governed by the Indian Child Welfare Act. This law was enacted to protect the rights of Indian children to be raised in an environment that reflects and respects their cultural values and mores. In addition, grandparents who are Native American or who have Native American grandchildren may have certain respite and financial resources available through tribal sources. As a result of the special applicability of the Indian Child Welfare Act and certain tribal resources, you should consult an attorney if you or your grandchild is Native American.

Preparing for the Unexpected

Despite all the precautions and special protections, you remain vulnerable. Just as some types of flu may attack you at unanticipated times, your rights and responsibilities as a grandparent are constantly changing. In addition to the issues discussed in this chapter, other unanticipated legal issues may arise that could affect your relationship with your grandchild.

For example, many seniors live in retirement communities that have restrictive covenants governing who may and may not live in a particular community. When you buy or rent housing in a community with such restrictive covenants, you agree to abide by these rules. Covenants that prevent children from living in the community may affect your ability to become your grandchild's primary caregiver. Before buying or renting housing in an area with restrictive covenants, you should have a lawyer experienced in real estate matters review the covenants and explain anything that you don't understand.

Another unanticipated legal issue is your ability to access senior services if you are accompanied by your grandchild. For example, some places that provide group meals for senior adults do not allow children to attend with their grandparents or to share meals. Rules such as these may restrict your ability to access some services or resources that you have traditionally relied upon.

Finally, if you become your grandchild's primary caregiver, it is very important that you plan for your grandchild's future. Because of the difference in age between you and your grandchild, there is a higher risk that you could lose the physical or mental capacity to continue to provide care for your grandchild, or you could die. Whether you are caring for your grandchild as a foster grandparent, a guardian, or a parent, you should consult an attorney and execute the appropriate documents to provide for the continued care and support of your grandchild in the event of your incapacity or death.

Under the laws of many states, the property of a person who dies without leaving a will or trust will be inherited by the deceased person's children. If you prefer that your grandchildren inherit your property upon your death instead of your children, you must have a document that is properly prepared and signed according to the laws of your state to ensure that your property passes according to your wishes.

Buyer Beware

If you decide to hire a professional to assist you in obtaining any of the rights or services discussed above, ask your friends or trusted advisors for references. Be sure to enter into a written contract describing the services to be provided and the fee you will be charged. Before signing the contract read it thoroughly. If the contract is not clear or you have any questions, ask to have the issues written in words you understand or ask another professional whether the proposed terms are fair and reasonable.

Do not rely on a verbal agreement for services. For example, if you are hiring a lawyer, be sure that the contract explains whether the lawyer will bill you a flat fee or an hourly rate, and whether expenses such as copying and court filing fees will be additional. You may be required to pay such expenses on a monthly basis even though the fee for services may not be owed until the services are complete.

What Does the Future Hold?

More grandparents than ever are raising their grandchildren, and this trend is expected to continue. As more of us become responsible for the daily care and well-being of our grandchildren, we will need to consider new forms of multigenerational housing and to develop social policies that address the needs of low-income grandparents caring for grandchildren. Get active. Help your community create a caring, supportive environment for you and your grandchildren.

Suggested Activities

- Find the contact information for your local aging agency and list the number here: _____.

- Go to the library (or use your home computer) and search the Internet to see if your state has any special information on the legal aspects of grandparenting.

- Ask your children to prepare and sign the appropriate medical consent forms or Powers of Attorney providing you with the authority to take action on behalf of your grandchildren if needed.

- Review your will or trust (or prepare one if you haven't already) to be sure that your grandchildren will continue to be cared for in the event of your death.

Prayer

God of the earth and the heavens, we realize that the laws of our country are based on your Holy Word. May we be sensitive to the spirit of the law and not just its traditions. Although there may be disagreements and heartaches, we pray that your grace and love will console us in these times. Help us to do what is right. Let us keep in mind what is best for grandchildren and their well-being. May grace abide in all that is deliberated and resolved in these difficult times. Amen.

chapter 10

GRANDPARENTS AND THEIR COLLEGE AGE GRANDCHILDREN

> CAST YOUR BREAD UPON THE WATERS,
> FOR AFTER MANY DAYS YOU WILL FIND IT
> AGAIN.
> ECCLESIASTES 11:1

Several years ago while touring a university in the Midwest, we had an opportunity to visit with a group of students in a fraternity. Several stories surfaced that proved insightful into the value of grandparents to their college age grandchildren. One of the frat members shared with the group about the difficulty he encountered in changing majors. He spoke of the strong commitment his dad had to engineering. In deference to his father, the young man had chosen engineering as his major, but found after a semester that this field of study was not for him. He loved his parents, which made it difficult to disappoint them by changing to a major in the liberal arts. This college student was not sure of how he might approach his parents.

One of his fraternity brothers suggested he talk to his grandparents about the situation. Up to now he had only sought help from faculty counselors and other students; even though they made helpful suggestions, none were satisfactory to him. No one up to this point had mentioned grandparents as a source of help. As soon as he could, he made arrangements to visit his grandparents. Upon arrival the student opened his heart and shared his emotional difficulties regarding a change in majors. As he spoke, there were tears running down his face. He was in a lot of pain and anxiety about the situation. His grandfather stood up, walked over to his grandson, put his arms around him, and said, "We can solve this problem together." While he was speaking with his grandfather, his grandmother brought him some homemade cookies with a glass of milk. They sat around, munching cookies and talking about his options. The grandparents, being the parents of this grandson's father, had considerable insight into the best way to tell his father about changing a major in the middle of freshman year.

After some discussion, they had a plan. The grandson was encouraged. Before the month was over the student invited his parents to spend the weekend with him at the university. Although the student was apprehensive about this time, he knew full well that his grandparents had found a way to discuss this issue with his parents. With great relief the young man was able to change majors without family conflict. He gave the credit to his grandparents for their wisdom in resolving a problem that seemed bigger than life to him. At this same meeting, another frat brother spoke to the group saying how much he wished he had grandparents to turn to in situations like this one. This is just one example of many where grandparents have literally "saved the day."

Joe, a student at a university in southern Missouri, was very interested in a very attractive young woman on campus. She was a student in the school of engineering where they were studying electronic developments in space exploration. He happened to mention to her that his grandfather was a retired professor of electrical engineering who had designed the communication system for the first moon landing. She was naturally anxious to meet Joe's grandfather. Joe invited his grandfather to campus and invited the pretty, young engineering student to dinner with the family. Needless to say, the evening went well. Most of the conversation was about the space program. Joe's grandfather was impressed with the young woman and encouraged Joe to "be good to her. She will make a fine granddaughter-in-law." One year later, Joe and the young woman were married and both are continuing to pursue graduate degrees.

In this chapter we examine ways the grandparenting career can be expanded to include grandchildren attending a college or university. To accomplish this goal, we will focus on the grandparents' unlimited possibilities for helping their grandsons or granddaughters during a time that is not only filled with fun and learning, but also may be filled with frustration, anxiety, and a sense of powerlessness.

As illustrated in the stories above, grandparents are becoming more important and more visible on college and university campuses throughout the country. A number of colleges and universities now have Grandparents' Day, Grandparents' Weekend, or Grandparents' Summer School, etc. One university in the Northeast has even developed a line of clothing especially for grandparents, sporting the college's logo and the word "Grandparent" on the front.

Likewise, colleges and universities are discovering significant financial benefits of recognizing grandparents. A college in the western part of the country invites grandparents to become a part of what they call "the Honors College Family." As colleges and universities see the numerous ways grandparents can benefit students, they are making every effort to include them in on-campus activities. Grandparents make valuable contributions as subscribers to college publications, as perennial contributors, and as supporters of sporting events. Research supports the above as more than a fad; it is a developing trend. With the multigenerational family and the life expectancy of grandparents exceeding two decades, we can expect an increasing number of grandparents and even great-grandparents to be more involved in their grandchildren's college careers. Families as well as higher education administrators are accepting and encouraging more than a placid role for the grandparents.

Consider the benefits that grandparents offer families with college age children as they pursue their academic degrees. Parents are often very busy earning the money to support children at home while making sure that their college age children have what they need. Grandparents often make the difference between the student's ability to stay in college and his or her need to drop out and take full-time employment. Also, as in the stories above, grandparents may be called upon to support their college grandchild who is struggling with questions about majors, choosing a mate, and many other serious decisions. This could include the decision of which college or university might be best suited for pursuing the grandchild's degree.

Universities and colleges are starting to recognize the importance of grandparents in their recruitment process as well. Many invite grandparents of prospective students to visit the campus for special activities with the hope that, with the grandparents' favorable impression, good students will enroll.

The majority of grandparents are familiar with the university scene. An increasing number have attended or graduated from college themselves. Some of the attributes grandparents have that are proving to be important to their grandchildren's college education are:

- Grandparents consistently name grandchildren at the top of their priority lists—thus distance, time, or responsibilities seldom get in the way of responding to their college age grandchildren.
- Grandparents are considered to be "safe" people. That is, non-judgmental, available, good listeners, and problem solvers.
- Grandparents who are religious consistently pray for their grandchildren. They also set an example integrating faith and knowledge, and help their grandchildren evaluate what they're learning in terms of their own faith commitments. This enables grandchildren to have balance and stability in a time when everything is changing so quickly.
- Grandparents can use their established networks to help identify and secure summer jobs for their college grandchildren. In addition to employment, networks offer other benefits such as new friends, new perspectives, and developing meaningful relationships outside the college or university environment.
- Grandparents may become friends with their grandchildren's classmates. This may help grandchildren to believe that their grandparents' support is authentic.

- Grandparents often take on partial or full responsibility for their grandchildren's financial needs.

- Grandparents are quick to affirm and celebrate both small and large successes of their grandchildren. The grandparents' presence at any recognition ceremony on campus provides a link between the college student and the rest of the family. Grandparents will pass on the recognition the grandchild receives. A grandparent's presence enhances the importance of the moment, even if other family members are present as well.

- Grandparents can often bridge the gap between their college grandchildren and the grandchildren's parents. Grandchildren in college often adopt dress codes and behaviors that are different from their parents' expectations. Grandparents can be an advocate for the grandchild and also help him understand the response of his parents. The bridge is two ways.

- Grandparents are there to lift up their grandchildren if setbacks occur, which they often do in the college years. Simply continuing to "be there," non-judgmentally, can be very significant when the grandchild has experienced a disappointment with a grade, a break-up with a girl or boy friend, etc.

- Grandchildren often see grandparents as good evaluators of the choices they are making in courses, majors, minors, or dates with whom they might become serious.

Up to now we have mentioned how grandparents help their grandchildren. Now let's look at some suggestions of the ways college and university grandchildren can encourage grandparents.

- Invite grandparents to campus activities. Very little will please your grandparents more than feeling that they are wanted at a campus activity with you.

- Recognize your grandparent's commitment to the family, which is often overlooked by other members. Grandparents love to discuss the family's history and have a strong desire to pass the family heritage on to you.

- Encourage your grandparents to become active or stay active in a faith based organization. Sometimes grandparents, for many reasons, drop out of their previous involvement with religious organizations. As a grandchild, you can help them recognize the value of spirituality and worship to their own well-being.

- Help your grandparents develop an interest in lifelong learning activities. As you become more involved and develop an appreciation of the benefits of learning, you might encourage grandparents to seize opportunities to attend classes and read materials that will enhance and add vitality to your grandparent's everyday lives.

- On weekends or summer visits, help with household chores that your grandparents may not be able to do or have overlooked. Not only does this help your grandparents, but it gives you a way to express appreciation for what they mean to you. It helps your grandparents know they will have someone who will be there for them in their time of need.

- Help grandparents develop new friends among younger age groups. Introducing your grandparents to your college age friends and professors can help them expand their range of intergenerational relationships.

- You can provide intellectual stimulation by your questions, suggested readings, and the cultural events you participate in. Often, college students are exposed to subjects and information that will be stimulating to grandparents and, perhaps, open a new world to them.

- Ask your grandparents about stories of how they met, raised your parents, and dealt with challenges over their lifetimes. This helps them feel that they've passed on a significant part of the family heritage. This is generally very important to grandparents and helps solidify their relationship with their grandchildren.

Guidelines

Be assertive in getting involved with your grandchildren in campus activities. Get a copy of the school calendar of events, usually available on the college or university website. If you don't have access to the Internet, ask your grandchildren to send a list of activities that might interest you. Talk over those events with your grandchildren and get their opinion about which ones would be best for you to attend. Knowing what's going on in terms of current events, entertainment, cultural events, and the like provides opportunities for conversations and shared interests.

When invited to share a campus activity with your grandchild, be quick to say yes and limit the questions regarding details of the invitation. When you ask too many questions, you're fulfilling the stereotype that is often associated with "old people." Trust your grandchildren to look out for you. Relax and enjoy this time with them.

Learn as much as possible about the college or university your grandchildren attend. Be aware of their major courses of study, their out-of-class activities and their schedule in general. Then you'll be able to tell your friends more about your grandchildren's college experience. Too often grandparents can only say to their friends that their grandchildren are *in* college.

Utilize e-mail as your primary form of communication. Students check their e-mail frequently each day, and it is a non-obtrusive way to keep in touch. As a result you will have more immediate responses and increased communication with your grandchildren.

Surprise your grandchildren by sending small gifts such as cookies, an interesting article, a joke, or a picture of your pet, for example. These surprise gifts need not be materialistic or expensive. The real gift in this gesture is your thoughtfulness and they will appreciate any gift from the "outside world."

Welcome not only your grandchildren into your home, but their roommates and other friends as well. Your grandchildren will appreciate knowing that you are willing to accept their friends. You will enjoy seeing how "grown up" your grandchild is.

Be sure to minimize complaining about infrequent visits or the length of time between visits. Your grandchildren will want to see you more often if their visiting experience is always as pleasant as you can make it. Avoid the mistake of "punishing" your grandchildren for not coming to see you more often. Scolding them will only make them want to avoid you more in the future.

Be willing to take risks. Don't worry about whether you win or lose but enjoy the experience. The only insurmountable activity, on a grandparent's weekend or visit to the campus, is the one you choose to avoid.

Maintain your physical and mental fitness. If you are fit, you should be able to enjoy a majority of campus activities without any problems. Even if you are physically challenged, there will be a number of activities you can enjoy. Trust your grandchildren to understand any limitations you have and they will love to help you adapt to almost any challenge.

Share your thoughts and love, not only by word of mouth but by actions. Some grandparents find it difficult to verbally express or even write loving feelings to their grandchildren. It is important, however, that you overcome any reluctance to share your feelings. This type of communication will surely draw you closer to your grandchildren.

Someone once said, "Life is too important to take seriously." Some think of grandparents as "sticks in the mud" because they seem fearful and reluctant to engage in laughter and fun activities. Trust God, yourself, and your grandchildren to see you through every encounter with every event.

Let your grandchildren help you. So often grandparents seem to think independence is a virtue. Thinking this way denies your grandchildren the privilege of giving back. They love you and one of the best things you can do for them is to allow them to show it by their helpful presence.

Laugh a lot. Share the funny things that happen to you daily, as well as jokes or cartoons that put a smile on your face. Laughter may be one of the better gifts you give your grandchildren.

Be yourself. What your grandchildren admire, respect, and love about you is found on the inside and not on the outside. Surely it is good to be well dressed, well groomed, and be "somebody." However, as grandparents, you are more than a "somebody." You have a unique place in your grandchild's life, and there's no one else like you.

Share your wisdom. Wisdom is the ability to use knowledge and experience to make good decisions. Understand that wisdom is far greater than knowledge or intelligence. Grandparents have experiences that have taught them how to recognize the difference between good and bad information. Godly grandparents have learned this from reading the wisdom literature of the Bible such as Proverbs, Ecclesiastes, and The Song of Solomon. Psalm 111:10 says that "The fear of the Lord is the beginning of wisdom, all who follow his precepts have good understanding."

Keep a journal of your experiences with your grandchildren during their college years. Along with your words, include pictures. Consider giving this to your grandchildren upon their graduation from college. It would be hard to beat this as a graduation gift.

Moving Forward: Suggestions

The college/university environment can be one of the most challenging, meaningful, and wonderful experiences anyone can have. This is especially true for grandparents. Consider the following:

- Think about the campus as a place where your grandchildren are encouraged to be themselves, share their ideas, develop new relationships, discover new knowledge, and gain an optimistic outlook.

- Expand your living space to include the college or university where your grandchildren attend, as well as including a college or university in your local community. You may find students who don't have grandparents who might be interested in you becoming a surrogate grandparent. Involving yourself with higher education helps you understand how to be involved in a career and not just an activity or event.

- Practice the guidelines in this chapter and share your thoughts about them with your family—especially your grandchildren.

The apostle Paul reminded the young minister Timothy of the benefits he received from his grandmother Lois (2 Timothy 1:5). Intergenerational discussions of family values and family history can prove to be invaluable to college students. This type of exchange is an investment that can provide many positive returns in the years ahead. As you evaluate your experiences with your grandchildren who are in college you will possibly join thousands of other grandparents who are reexperiencing (some for the first time) college and consider becoming a perennial student.

Prayer

Heavenly Father, we grandparents want to see our grandchildren grow intellectually, physically, and spiritually. Please help us to be wise in the ways we relate to them as they pursue their education and training during their young adult years. May our lives be examples of your grace, and may our words be guided by the Holy Spirit. Amen.

chapter 11

SURROGATE GRANDPARENTING

> LIVE WISELY...AND MAKE THE MOST OF EVERY OPPORTUNITY. LET YOUR CONVERSATION BE GRACIOUS AND EFFECTIVE SO THAT YOU WILL HAVE THE RIGHT ANSWER FOR EVERYONE.
>
> COLOSSIANS 4:5-6 (NLT)

> THERE FOLLOWETH AFTER ME TODAY A YOUTH WHOSE FEET WILL PASS THIS WAY. THIS STREAM, WHICH HAS BEEN AS NAUGHT TO ME, TO THAT FAIR-HAIRED BOY MAY A PITFALL BE; HE, TOO, MUST CROSS IN THE TWILIGHT DIM— GOOD FRIEND, I AM BUILDING THIS BRIDGE FOR HIM.
>
> W. A. DROMGOOLE

Every kid in the neighborhood calls him "Pop." He has a shop in his garage and tinkers with a variety of woodworking activities. He makes his living hiring out as a general handyman. To the boys and girls in the community he is more than a tinkerer. He fills a void in their lives as a grandfather figure. Most of the families in that neighborhood do not live close to the children's biological grandparents. In reality, he is a surrogate grandfather to the children because *they* have adopted him. This is one way people become surrogate grandparents. Pop seems to always have time to speak to the children and tell them stories. If any of them falls and skins a knee they will run to Pop who keeps a first aid box handy in his tool cabinet. He feels that he is simply a part of the "village" that is responsible for raising the young. Pop's example is a modern illustration of the African proverb stated above. He was faithfully contributing to the raising of the children in his community.

The story of Eli and Samuel in the Bible illustrates an important role for the surrogate grandparent. Samuel's parents dedicated him to the Lord and placed him in the care of the priest, Eli. Eli, although very old, took charge of the young boy and provided care and instruction. As a result Samuel became one of the greatest prophets in the history of Israel (1 Samuel 2-3).

Types of Foster Grandparents

There are at least two types of surrogate, or foster, grandparents: Formal and informal. Some seek the role and become involved with organizations such as the *National Foster Grandparent* program. We would call these *formal* surrogate grandparents. Others are designated as grandparent figures, informally, by their relationship with the children of their neighborhoods, churches, or organizations. For example, one older man whose biological grandchildren lived hundreds of miles away, would carry candy in his pockets that he would give to children and their parents when they came to Sunday school. It was his delight to see the children run to him when he came in the door of the church. He made sure that it was okay with the parents to give candy to their children by giving a piece of candy to the parents as well. Often he would volunteer to help with the younger children during what the church called the "extended session" (the period of time after Sunday school when the parents were in a formal worship service). Most of the time he simply sat in a chair in the preschool department where his presence seemed to have a calming effect on the children.

A church in a small southern town asked the president of the local bank to become their first "Sunday School Granddaddy." His three-year-old grandson was one of the children in the preschool department. At first the people were reluctant to ask such an important man to assume such a menial job, but they noticed that he spent a great deal of time with his grandson. He agreed to accept the position on a trial basis for one month. He would walk around in the room where two-, three-, and four-year-olds were playing and listening to stories. He would hold his grandson and another child on his knees while he read to them from a children's Bible story book. After a month, he decided to stay. Even after his grandson moved on to the older children's department, he stayed on as the Sunday School Granddaddy in the preschool department.

The two stories above illustrate how serving as a helper in the church and community can be as vital to the lives of children as one who preaches from the pulpit or teaches Sunday school lessons. Edgar Guest wrote a powerful poem that highlights this truth: "I'd rather see a sermon than hear one any day; I'd rather one should walk with me than merely tell the way. The eye's a better pupil and more willing than the ear. Fine counsel is confusing, but example's always clear..."[31]

Some older persons volunteer to work in children's hospitals where they make sure that every child has a grandparent type who notices them and makes children who are ill feel they are not alone when their parents are not present. Jerry, a seven-year-old boy, fell out of a tree and broke several bones. His parents both worked outside the home and could not be with him during the day. Mrs. Cranford, a neighbor from across the street, volunteered to stay with Jerry at the hospital while his parents were at work. She had known him since he was a baby. In fact, Jerry called her "Nanna Cranford" because she was a lot like his grandmother who lived in another state.

Some surrogate grandparents volunteer to help with such groups as Boy Scouts, Girl Scouts, 4H Clubs, and Big Brothers and Big Sisters. And some work with Charles Colson's *Angel* program[32] at Christmas time and then continue to make regular visits with the children of people who are incarcerated in local, state, and federal prisons. In the Angel program, the surrogate grandparent "angel" receives a list of children with specific requests for Christmas presents and then delivers those presents on behalf of the children's parents. These surrogate grandparents also make contact with the children's parents in prison and provide an invaluable service by enabling reentry of the parents into their children's lives.

Adopt-a-grandparent programs, often associated with nursing homes, may also be called a surrogate grandparent activity. Adolescents from local churches, high schools and colleges often derive significant benefit from establishing relationships with residents in extended care facilities.

---

31 http://www.sofinesjoyfulmoments.com/quotes/sermon.html
32 http://www.angeltree.org/contentindex.asp?ID=64

Surrogate grandparenting doesn't happen just by yourself. You can get involved in senior centers that provide surrogate grandparenting activities. Churches and civic organizations are other options where you can find surrogate grandparenting with young people in their communities. Military units sometimes take on projects of providing needed services for needy children and their families.

Why would someone seek to become a surrogate grandparent? There are probably as many reasons as there are people who volunteer for this role. One reason is that humans are primarily relational beings. We all need bonded type relationships with other people. There's something special about relationships between "grandparent types" and children. People who have lost a significant person in their life may desire to fill that emotional void with a surrogate grandparenting relationship. In other situations the grandchildren have grown up and the grandparents haves a special desire to work with children who remind them of special times spent with their own biological grandchildren. Another reason may be that they have retired from a position that required most of their time and they now have a vacancy in their lives that they are seeking to fill. Surrogate grandparenting becomes their new career. People may recall someone helping them when they were young and they remember how important that help was to their lives and they wish to give a child a similar opportunity. Joining a foster grandparent group provides a strong sense of belonging to something very important and they are able to engage in meaningful social activities as well. This involvement creates a needed sense of community.

Foster Grandparents as Friends

One of the most important motives that keeps people involved in surrogate grandparenting is friendship. As in the illustrations above, friends are where we find them. We do not usually go out looking for friends; they just seem to happen as we engage in interactions with people in our everyday lives. Foster grandparents who become involved in the lives of lonely or needy children often make lifelong friends with them. New friends often come from encounters beyond our comfort zones. Vulnerability and trust are important qualities that are prerequisite to making new friends. Trust gives one a sense of security, i.e., experiences can be shared with one another knowing that a friend will keep the conversation private, listen well, and be a reliable source of support regardless of the circumstances. Before people can allow themselves to be vulnerable, they must be able to trust and feel that they are free from scripting.

Psychologists have identified four levels or types of friendships. It is important for surrogate grandparents to understand that there are differences in the scripted expectations for each of them.

On the first level we can classify the majority of our acquaintances as friends. These are people who live in our city or suburb, or rural community, and who we normally do not have a great deal of interaction with.

The people at church, work, or those who live in the immediate neighborhood may constitute a second, somewhat closer type of friendship. Interaction is limited but friendly.

A third level is with people we enjoy visiting and whose presence "makes the party better." We are always glad to see them.

The fourth and most intimate level of friendship is with a few people with whom we would be vulnerable, i.e., we would not hesitate to share our deepest secrets with them. The surrogate grandparent may become a fourth-level friend to a surrogate grandchild, but this does not necessarily imply that the grandparent feels compelled to reciprocate this level of vulnerability with the grandchild. Don't expect this level of friendship to begin immediately. Most often there is a progression through the levels before the fourth level is achieved.

Characteristics of Surrogate Grandparents

Some of the key characteristics or qualities of people who engage in surrogate grandparenting are:

- They have an interest in giving back.
- They have experienced a life that leads them to want to reach out and help others.
- They may be male, female or any age or ethnic group.
- They relate to others with ease.
- Unlimited time is not necessarily a prerequisite. Some surrogate grandparents who have busy schedules can also be effective.
- Surrogate grandparents are generally community minded. They participate in community activities that benefit others in a variety of settings.
- There are no economic requirements. Both the wealthy and less wealthy may be qualified.
- They are open to lifelong learning activities.
- They have a concern for the young. For most, their own spirituality is a primary motivator for becoming a surrogate grandparent.

- They've learned through experience and education certain skills that may be helpful to their surrogate grandchildren.
- They have hobbies and craft skills they can enjoy and share with surrogate grandchildren.
- They have the ability to listen.
- Our observation of hundreds of surrogate grandparents reveals that they have a love of America and they freely share this value with their surrogate grandchildren.
- Transportation is not a necessary prerequisite.

A Model of Formal Surrogate Grandparenting

One of the best models of surrogate grandparenting is the *National Foster Grandparent Program*.[33] A government publication created a number of years ago captured the spirit of foster grandparents. The Corporation for National and Community Service invited children in successful foster grandparent relationships to provide works of art, poems, and messages for a special brochure. The response to this request was overwhelming but only a few of the children's works were chosen to be included in the brochure. One child (speaking about a foster grandmother) said, "She makes me think of a beautiful rainbow with me under it." Another one said, "I love my grandmother as much as I love my chickens." A young man, speaking of his foster grandfather, said, "The most important thing he showed me is: Never give up!" The most moving message from a child to foster grandparents was, "Without you there'd be a space in my heart empty and lonely with no place to start."

---

33   http://www.seniorcorps.gov/about/programs/fg.asp

Foster Grandparents, a federally funded program, has an abundance of foster grandparents who serve approximately four hours per day in halfway houses, hospital wards, detention centers, special schools, and institutions. The children they foster may be troubled, confused, blind, deaf, in wheelchairs, or they may have learning and physical challenges. A statement from the *Foster Grandparent Program* says it best: "This program provides a chance for old and young Americans to answer each other's needs and get to know each other." Essentially, the *Foster Grandparent Program* has been so successful it can be duplicated in almost any community. Its focus gives older grandparents opportunities for growth, purpose, and fulfillment. Witnessing the work of *Foster Grandparent* volunteers leaves you with a strong belief that this particular kind of career gives them a reason to live, and to love, a relationship best illustrated by a short poem written by an unknown foster grandparent attending the Woody Cooper National Grandparent Jamboree:

A Time-Tested Recipe to Live and Share

Take one grandparent

Add one Child

Mix in a heap of Love

Fold in several Hugs

Stir in a lot of Caring

Sprinkle with Tears and Laughter

Blend weekly

Yield a life time of Joy

—Author unknown

The *Foster Grandparenting* program is so meaningful throughout the country that there are waiting lists of older people wishing to become foster grandparents. As you may recall, this was one of Nancy Reagan's favorite programs.

Important Considerations

During these turbulent times there is considerable news about adults who abuse children of all ages. In light of this visibility a word of caution is in order. Whenever you are interested or may begin a grandparenting relationship, be careful to visit first with parents and friends of the youth you wish to help. Don't be insulted if you are asked to have a criminal check. Almost anyone involved with youth today take this step, not only to satisfy other people, but to provide protection for the foster grandparent. Always get permission from those in authority to involve youth with any activity. What we have just said should not be considered a deterrent to becoming a surrogate grandparent. It is more a reflection of the times. If you have questions about this precaution, check with your pastor, legal counselor, or a youth services worker. They can and will provide you with helpful information that will protect you and the youth. They can also provide you with insight into the best way to relate to young people.

When you first start spending time with your surrogate grandchild, it might be best to have other people present. It might even be more enjoyable to team up with another surrogate grandparent and talk about how you can work together and share ideas.

Think of surrogate grandparenting as similar to *Big Brother/Big Sisters*. It might even be helpful to contact this organization for a visit and see how that programs works.

It is important that you err on the side of caution, but not on the side of neglect. Hopefully, this discussion of surrogate grandparenting has given you a new perspective of this important relationship. Perhaps you've never considered yourself as a surrogate grandparent. It is our hope that you can now identify and consider some of the opportunities to be a surrogate grandparent in your community. True, it may be risky, but the rewards exceed any consequences of risking. This is a much needed assignment in reaching children of all ages in the 21st century. Please be among that number that steps forward and makes a difference in another person's life. Go for it!!!

Prayer

Father in Heaven, thank you for the youth we have the privilege to serve. They have renewed our spirit and my desire more than ever before to be what they need us to be. Help us be better listeners, better friends and most of all, better grandparents for them. May our "grandchildren" see Jesus in my words and actions for them as well as others. Amen.

chapter 12

LONG DISTANCE GRANDPARENTING

> EVEN WHEN I AM OLD AND GRAY, DO NOT FORSAKE ME, O GOD, TILL I DECLARE YOUR POWER TO THE NEXT GENERATION, YOUR MIGHT TO ALL WHO ARE TO COME.
> PSALM 71:18 NIV

> THE BEST AND MOST BEAUTIFUL THINGS IN THE WORLD CANNOT BE SEEN, OR EVEN TOUCHED; THEY MUST BE FELT WITH THE HEART.
> HELEN KELLER

I am separated from my grandchildren by over 600 miles. I only get to see them three or four times a year if I'm lucky. Being separated frustrates me because my six grandchildren are growing up without me, and the relationship I want with them is largely undeveloped. Frankly, this unacceptable dilemma is the primary reason for writing this chapter. Perhaps you will find ways to draw closer to your "distance" grandchildren as I share my insights. Researchers Cherlin and Fursteinberg describe three types of grandparents: involved, companionate, and remote.[34] In the terms of the above research, my relationship with my grandchildren is remote.

Distance is taking on new meanings. There was a time when we considered going across town a major trip. Many of us remember taking a bus from one part of town to another. We would have to transfer when we reached the center of town. Likewise, in the past, traveling from one state to another seemed overwhelming. Older generations thought of crossing state lines like we think of going to another country today. Maybe you remember when you were only allowed to ride your bike on your block. When you were allowed to ride your bike to school three or four blocks away, it was a major trip. The first time you got to drive the family car by yourself was almost like Columbus discovering the new world.

Our understanding of distance has changed immensely in the last few years. Now interstate super highways, air travel, and rapidly developing technology are shrinking distance to where it is no longer defined in terms of miles, but hours, or even seconds. How long will it be before we can say "beam me over" and we will be there instantly? What was science fiction a few years ago is to a great extent reality today. "Around the world in 80 days" seems like a long tedious journey compared to the ability of new super-sonic airplanes to travel the distance in a matter of hours instead of days. If science and technology have accomplished so much in such a short time, isn't it possible for grandparents in this high-tech world to make the same type of progress?

---

34 A. J. Cherlin and F. Furstenberg, "Grandparents and Family Crisis," *Generations*, Vol. 10, 1986.

Distance is relative. While families living in the same neighborhood may feel that the distance between their members is considerable, others who live in different states or across the country are able to maintain relatively close relationships. Now, the term distance transcends physical description and includes spiritual, cultural, social, psychological, educational and legal properties.

In this chapter we'll discuss different types of "long distances" grandparents face in society. Hopefully as a result, you will no longer see distance as a barrier. For most of us, love is the driving force that motivates us to enter airports and cyberspace to be with our grandchildren.

Distance Redefined

Dictionaries define distance in several ways: *Physical distance*, which refers to separation in space and time; *social distance*, which is about remoteness in relationships; *emotional distance*, which describes being at a mental or emotional distance from someone; and *spiritual distance*, which has reference to the deferential of intensity in faith and values.

Besides miles, there are a number of non-physical things keeping grandparents and grandchildren at a distance:

- *Generation gap:* Two generations seem to be in different worlds.
- *Divorce and remarriage*: Sometimes grandparents are left out.
- *Working grandparents:* Employment of either or both grandparents makes it difficult to spend much time with or to think about the grandchildren.

- *Mobile families*: Children and grandchildren move often, such as those in the military, and regular communication is difficult.

- *Living arrangements*: Grandparents move to a retirement community or nursing home and long-distance communication methods appear limited.

- *Physical decline*: Grandparents become writing or hearing impaired.

- *Conflict within the family:* Communication is purposely cut off or severely limited.

- *Technologically deprived*: Grandparents do not have access to a computer and perhaps limited use of the telephone.

- *Financial challenges*: Grandparents do not have enough money to spend on travel or expensive communication devices.

- *Chronic busyness*: Grandparents or grandchildren think that they are "too busy" to make the effort to remain in touch and grow in relationship.

- *Ageism*: Grandparents and grandchildren, because of age, may feel they live in different worlds.

- *Religious differences*: There are contradictions in the integration of faith.

Solutions to Overcoming Distance Challenges

Distance in miles. John and Mary live in Dallas, Texas. Their two grandchildren, who are twelve and nine, live with their parents in San Antonio 274 miles away. Travel between the two families is not prohibitive—about five hours on the road, but distance makes it difficult for them to often be together. When the grandparents do visit, they enjoy watching their grandchildren's sports activities or school programs. Mary also enjoys going to one of the grandchildren's schools and reading a book to the class or helping as a volunteer on Grandparents' Day. At such events they take many pictures and give the child an album to remember the occasion.

Despite the distance, John and Mary have discovered ways to keep close to their beloved grandchildren. They call weekly. Every few weeks Mary writes a brief encouraging letter to each of the grandchildren. She encloses cartoons and sayings clipped from various publications. For example, if she knows that her grandchild is having trouble with reading, she says, "Your daddy had trouble with reading in the third grade too. But, with practice he got better by the end of the year." She also clipped a cartoon where a Peanuts character is having the same trouble. Sometimes she sends coloring books or puzzles when the children are sick to lift their spirits. Likewise, the grandchildren reward their grandparents with their works of art or lessons showing good grades. For several years, John and Mary, as part of the extended family, have taken a trip to the hill country in Wyoming for a week of family fun. On these occasions, their grandchildren have learned to ski, to fish, and to hike.

Distance due to work. Carl and Sue are in their mid 50s and live in Grand Forks, North Dakota. He holds a responsible position at the Air Force base while she is a professor at the university. Both live busy lives and look forward to retirement. Their son and daughter-in-law, along with their nine-year-old granddaughter Eve, live in Nashville, Tennessee. Their careers demand much time and energy.

Carl and Sue, as a result, have little time or energy. However, they are determined to remain close to their son and his family, especially Eve.

Carl and Sue are familiar with computers and software programs. There are computer packages that include software, phones and web cameras, which enable Carl and Sue to stay close. They can see and talk with their grandchildren in real time. This special event usually takes place on Saturday afternoons. Eve also likes to have email dialogue with her grandparents.

Last summer on her ninth birthday, Eve flew to Grand Forks and spent a week with her grandparents. They have a house in the country overlooking the Red River. Carl taught Eve how to fish; in fact, Eve caught the biggest fish. Her favorite activity was feeding the cows. One of the cows had a two-month-old calf. Eve loved to feed and pet the calf. The calf was multicolored so she named it Rainbow. There seemed to be a chemistry between Rainbow and Eve, especially at feeding time. When the week was up, Carl and Sue flew back to Nashville with Eve and spent several days with their adult children and grandchild. Their "piggyback" trip went so well, Carl and Sue plan to do it again this summer.

Distance due to chronic busyness. Thelma is a 70-year-old widow who is trying to stay as busy as she can to cover up her grief at the death of her husband two years earlier. She has become active in her church's senior adult ministry, especially in taking bus trips to interesting places. She enjoys fellowship with other Christians, many of whom have experienced similar losses in their lives. Six months ago, Thelma learned to play bridge and has been invited to be a part of a bridge group that meets twice a week.

Since the death of her husband, it appears that Thelma's 16-year-old granddaughter Lucy has taken a back seat. Lucy lives thirty minutes away at a boarding school for girls. Thelma and Lucy used to be close. In fact, Lucy wanted to go to this particular boarding school because her grandparents lived nearby. While her grandfather was ill, Lucy often spent weekends with her grandparents, trying to help. Now that her grandfather is gone and Thelma is filling her life with other things, they do not often see each other. Hopefully, when Thelma has worked through her grief, this distance will be bridged. In the meantime their spiritual bond is unconsciously sustaining the relationship.

What makes the difference between families? Some grandparents, despite the challenges, remain close to their grandchildren; others do not. In our three examples, two sets of grandparents were highly motivated to have an intimate relationship with their grandchildren. They did what they could with the time they had to be active participants in their grandchildren's lives. As evidenced by their selfless actions, they were motivated by their love for their children and grandchildren. Because they loved, they put forth the necessary effort to develop the relationship. Also, perhaps they remembered the special relationship they had had with their grandparents and wanted the same for their grandchildren.

Even though one can appreciate Thelma's grief and her efforts to survive, her method of dealing with loss has become selfish. She has turned inward and is no longer aware or concerned about her granddaughter who lives nearby. If she had given Lucy a chance to be near her, the situation probably would have brought them closer than ever before. Instead, Thelma allowed her grief to undermine her relationship with her granddaughter.

Getting Started on a Grandparenting Program

Becoming an involved long-distant grandparent isn't easy and does not happen by chance. Some things you try will succeed, others will not. Sometimes you may need to leave your comfort zone. Many older adults have forgotten how to play. Learn again how to relate with a child or a teenager. There is risk involved. Some of your attempts to draw near your grandchildren may be spurned. Grandparenting by nature must be creative and fluid if the relationship is to develop.

Bridging the gap between the grandparents and grandkids will take place if some initial steps are taken. First, grandparents must decide to be close to their grandchildren no matter the distance between them. It will be helpful if they talk with their adult children, asking how they can be a part of the ongoing functioning of the family. Discuss characteristics of the grandchildren—their strengths and weakness, their interests, their needs, school, sports, and whatever else that might be considered relevant.

Your efforts in expanding your long-distance grandparenting skills will inevitably make you aware of some challenges. Stan Merrill cites several of these:

- Staying informed about your grandchildren's lives
- Traveling to spend time with your grandchildren
- Remembering your grandchildren on special occasions
- Knowing what to talk about
- Passing on your family history and values
- Helping your grandchildren with their problems
- Having adequate time and energy to stay in touch

- Being an effective grandparent while keeping other commitments[35]

Motivation for Grandparenting

Perhaps you can identify with some of my motives. I know what it's like to have great parents, but somehow I missed the grandparent-grandchild relationship. Most everyone says that this relationship is wonderful. The bumper sticker says, "If I had known how great grandchildren were, I would have skipped the kids." It's difficult for me to identify with those emotions. I did not know my grandparents very well, but I want my six grandkids to know me and to know my love for them.

God apparently intended that children have an extended family. With greater longevity, five generations are now possible within a family. The traditional family unit is dad, mom, and children. But it is even better when children know their grandparents and maybe their great-grandparents. Older generations often can share family stories and pass on their faith and morals. The support and encouragement of the third and fourth generations to the youngest can provide a safety net and set the path for the grandchildren to follow. I want my grandchildren to know their roots and experience the support of loving grandparents. As Solomon once said about the support of mutual friends, "Though one may be overpowered, two can defend themselves. A cord of three strands is not quickly broken" (Ecclesiastes 4:12). When grandchildren know that they have the support of their grandparents they will be able to endure almost any hardship that comes their way.

---

35   Stan W. Merrill, *Seven Activities You Can Do with Your Grandchildren When They're a Thousand Miles Away*, www.DearGrandkids.com, 2006.

Your story and your relationship with your family are probably different than mine, but I believe you and I share some of the same motives. Let's get to know our grandchildren and be a part of their lives, even with those who are separated from us. I think we'll find that being at a distance can actually be a blessing. Since we're not close, communicating with them by phone, computer, and letter are methods that lend themselves to more person-to-person contact.

Ways to Stay in Touch

Being together in person. The most effective way to develop a relationship with our distant grandchildren is to be with them in person, either by visiting in each other's homes or by traveling together. My daughter told me recently that the one two-week trip she made with my wife's parents did more for their relationship than anything else they ever did. When you visit in your adult children's home or they are in yours, make sure that your schedule includes some alone time with each grandchild. Planning ahead of time is necessary for making those memorable occasions significant.

Mail. Getting something in the mail from grandparents can be exciting for children. It is something they can hold in their hands and examine over and over again. Here are some ideas.

- Send your grandchild stationery, preaddressed labels, and postage stamps so they can respond to your letters and not be slowed down by a lack of writing material or stamps.
- Send a care package with snacks (approved by their parents), a small gift, and perhaps a picture when you were their age.

- Share things in a letter about what is going on in your life and ask them to do the same.[36]

Telephone calls. Calling your grandchildren on the telephone is a great way to communicate. Be sure you talk with them one-on-one. It will make your grandchild feel special. However, if using the telephone is to be a regular part of your communication strategy, it is good to answer some questions ahead of time.

- When is the best time of the day to call so it doesn't interrupt your children's family schedule?
- How often should you call?
- How much money can you spend each month on telephone calls?
- Can your grandchildren call you collect (if collect calls are possible)?
- What subjects would interest your grandchildren?
- What questions might you ask that would encourage your grandchildren to open up and tell you about their world?[37]

The telephone will also enable you to do some things WITH your grandchildren. When you have experiences together, it deepens the relationship, especially when you hear their laughter, questions, and joy. Consider the following:

- Read a bedtime story over a speakerphone.

---

36 Ann Feenstra, *Long-Distance Grandparenting*, www.lifeway.com.
37 C. Corson, K. DeHart, S. Bowman and A. J. Walker, *Grandparenting from a Distance*, Oregon State University Extension Service, March, 2001.

- Cook something parallel with your grandchild, where you both have the same recipe and ingredients and do it together over the speakerphone. (Recipes may be found online at places like www.easy-kids-recipes.com or www.familyfun.go.com.)
- Play a network computer game with your grandchild.
- With the telephone on, visit a virtual museum together, such as:

    - Thomas Jefferson's home, Monticello (www.monticello.org)
    - The ancient civilizations site at the British Museum (www.ancientcivilizations.co.uk)
    - The interactive activities at the Seattle Art Museum (www.seattleartmuseum.org/Learn/Teach/LearnOnline.asp)[38]

- Call after a sporting event that both you and your grandchild enjoy watching on television, or after a special happening at school or church.[39]

Technology provides a vast number of ways to communicate and things to do with your grandchildren. Some require learning new skills, such as using email and the Internet. Whatever your level of expertise, do what works best for you and your grandchildren. Most kids in our country become familiar with technology early in life. Using it will help you be a part of their world.

---

38   Merrill, *Seven Activities*
39   Loma G. D. Silcott, *Long Distance Grandparenting: Tips on Staying in Touch*, www.grandtimes.com.

Computers. Computers will enable you and your grandchildren to write email to each other. One wonderful thing about email is that your messages arrive almost instantly and often are waiting for them when they turn on the computer. New webcam technology makes it possible to see your grandchildren while you are talking over the Internet. Here are a few more ideas:

- How about creating a homepage on the World Wide Web where you can post pictures, family history, jokes, and other fun things for your grandchildren? This is an excellent interactive and ongoing project.

- Hallmark on its website allows you to pick e-cards (i.e., greeting cards that are usually animated), personalize them, and send them to your grandchildren free of charge.

- There are many instant messaging (IM) programs out there that allow you to send and receive messages instantaneously as if you were verbally talking to each other. Your grandchildren can probably tell you about the latest devices that are available and being used by young and old alike.

Faxes. If both grandparents and grandchildren have a fax, then they can easily send material back and forth to each other. One grandmother shipped fax machines to each of her children so that all the grandkids could communicate with her. She wanted to help them with their homework, send them little encouraging notes two or three mornings a week, and stay in touch. She encouraged sharing their homework, jokes, report cards, art work, and whatever else.

Videos and audio tapes. Older technology like tape recorders and video recorders can be used to enrich communication and relationships with grandchildren.

- Find a good children's book your grandchildren would enjoy and tape record yourself reading it. Then mail them the book and tape.

- Videotape yourself working in the garden, going on an outing, or taking an interesting trip and mail it to the grandkids. As you tape it, narrate by talking to your grandchildren and mention them by name. It will make them feel like they are actually there.

- Your adult children can videotape your grandchildren's special events at school, church, or extracurricular activities and share them with you.[40]

Modern technology enables you to be just a "click" away from your grandchildren who may live hundreds of miles away or may be separated from you for other reasons. You can now be close from a distance. Telephones, computers, fax machines, audio and video recorders, and mail allow you to be up close and personal with each grandchild. All you need is planning, time, energy, and creative imagination. Then you can experience closeness with your grandchildren. Some things will be a drain; other activities will energize. Loving and knowing your grandchildren will add life to your years, and it will give encouragement and support to your grandchildren.

---

40 Feenstra, *Long-Distance Grandparenting*.

Suggestions for Shortening Long-Distance Grandparenting

- Make a commitment to stay close to your grandchildren who are far away.

- Use modern technology—such as email, texting, and instant messaging—to communicate with grandchildren on a regular basis.

- Use older technology—such as mail, fax machines, tape recorders, camcorders, and telephones—to share your world and have fun with your grandchildren.

- Use modern travel conveniences to visit or travel with grandchildren as often as possible.

Enabling Activities

- Make a list of different ways in which you can communicate with grandchildren living at a distance.

- After reviewing this chapter, make a list of things you can do with each avenue of communication.

- Share this information with your adult children and seek the best ideas for drawing closer to your grandchildren.

- Make a plan for improving communication with your grandchildren.

- After the first six months of intentionally drawing closer to your grandchildren, evaluate and discuss with your adult children progress made in relationships.

Prayer

Dear Heavenly Father, thank you for blessing our lives with grandchildren. You made each one unique and special. Help us, Father, to make them feel special by the way we treat them. Some of us live many miles away; some are separated for other reasons. Our prayer is that those barriers which hinder our being close may one day soon be overcome. May our love for them motivate us to spend the necessary time and energy to figure out ways to be with them, whether it is over the telephone or the Internet or even in person. Give us the wisdom to find avenues through which we might get to know them better. In Jesus name we pray. Amen.

chapter 13

Grandparenting Today and Tomorrow

> Don't copy the behavior and customs of this world, but let God transform you into a new person by changing the way you think. Then you will know what God wants you to do, and you will know how good and pleasing and perfect his will really is.
>
> Romans 12:2 NLT

Who ever would have thought of grandparenting as being something more than a role? A role that often meant the grandparent was "putty" that patched up the "leaks" and "holes" in the family dam. Today and tomorrow, grandparenting is and will no longer be viewed as a temporary "plug" in the family structure. It will now take its place as one of the most important rapidly growing careers in this country. The grandparenting career evolved out of a rich heritage. One of the best examples of this process is a story about a grandmother who held strong Christian beliefs and the sacredness of life, believing that God has a purpose for every living human being. This grandmother more than a decade ago provided the "putty" necessary to help a young man know and understand what love is. This grandchild had been born to parents who were addicted to alcohol and other narcotics. They frequently brought this child to the grandmother's home. Through her steadfastness, strong faith, and incalculable love this woman raised Bruce Bowen, one of the best known professional basketball players of our time. A staff writer for the June 10, 2007, *Denver Post* told this story. In her reporting she underscored the importance that Bowen's religious foundation and grandmother provided for him. As a consequence he is much more than one of the best professional basketball players in the National Basketball Association. He complements his basketball career with his devotion to youth in San Antonio, Texas.

Bruce often takes time to read to children at various community centers in the city. His story is not that unusual. Millions of grandparents, both men and women, have contributed in the same way as this basketball star's grandmother.

Having a grandparenting career provides greater recognition, more respect, and an increased amount of support from governmental and nongovernmental agencies. For example, the Older American's Act, in Title I where the Objectives of the Act are outlined, makes no mention of grandparenting. Hopefully, the next time this life-changing act is amended legislators will recognize grandparenting as a legitimate and irreplaceable part of the family structure. As most of you know, Hallmark Cards has attempted to recognize and celebrate grandparents by designating a certain weekend in September as Grandparents' Day. Their efforts have been met with little success. Churches, schools, civic clubs, fraternal orders, and other family supporting organizations have yet to understand that grandparenting is now a career.

The purpose of this book has been to take a closer look, both subjectively and objectively, at grandparenting in this society. As you have read, there are many grandparenting types. Only a few have been identified, described, and discussed in this book.

Summary of the Chapters

You may recall a chapter about single grandparenting gave emphasis to the large number of single grandparents in our society. We outlined both challenges and opportunities singles face and gave suggestions to help you adapt to your grandparenting career. Although little has been written about single grandparents, we are confident that you can find comfort and strength in your relationship with God. The apostle Paul underscores this belief in Romans 11:33: "Oh, what a wonderful God we have! How great are his riches and wisdom and knowledge!..." (NLT).

Another chapter discussed the relationship grandparents have with their adult children. Differences in lifestyles and child rearing often make it stressful for all involved. But the difficulties are solvable. We gave recommendations to facilitate meaningful relationships in the family. Lance Robertson guest-contributed a chapter on grandparents parenting their grandchildren. He shared his story about his grandparents raising him and how they affected his entire life. Other stories were also shared about other grandparents raising their grandchildren and struggles they faced with financial, physical, and emotional resources. It would be hard to find any of these individuals parenting their grandchildren who would say anything other than, "It was worth the investment and I would do it again."

Another contributor, Jim Hughes, was invited to write on distance grandparenting. Jim's story hits home with thousands of individuals who are separated from their beloved grandchildren. Jim gives us a closer look at the trials, the hurts, and many efforts employed to overcome geographical distances. He speaks of different types of distances and concludes there are distances other than miles that can make people feel a long way from their grandchildren. Jim's faith and knowledge of computers played an important role in overcoming not only geographical distances, but other kinds of distances. He provided suggestions to assist anyone attempting to draw closer to their grandchildren.

Blended families and the complexity of grandparenting in their social environment could have been an entire book. After discussing the issues with a number of grandparents in blended families, we identified and discussed possible frictions among a number of grandparents, all wanting to do the right thing with their grandchildren. Other than single grandparenting, grandparenting in blended families is a category where the majority of grandparents find themselves. Helpful hints are provided for overcoming some of the stressful situations grandparents in blended families encounter.

One very interesting chapter is on the importance of ethnicity in grandparenting. We identified and described several ethnic groups as well as how ethnicity is a resource that enriches grandchildren's lives. We believe that all grandparents can find value in reviewing the unique lessons their own ethnic background provides and in passing those lessons on to their grandchildren. Grandparents from all backgrounds can also gain insight and skills from observing the rich heritage of other ethnic groups.

Spiritual development is another chapter the authors had difficulty bringing to a close. With one of the authors being a theologian, greater insight was possible through his knowledge of the scriptures and the importance of religious education. Even though readers of this book may come from different faith traditions, we discussed the topic in such a way that emphasizes God's love and how essential it is to draw on one's spiritual resources.

Grandparenting college and university students is often thought of as a career where grandparents manifest the pride and pleasure they have in their young adult grandchildren. Very seldom discussed are the additional responsibilities grandparents have during their grandchildren's college years. In this chapter we emphasized the fact that grandparents can be among the safest people and provide safe situations for their grandchildren. Grandparents of college and university students are generally characterized by their nonjudgmental responses and acceptance of their grandchildren no matter what the circumstances.

Surrogate grandparenting is not as visible as many of the other grandparenting types. As discussed in this chapter, grandparents in the surrogate career may take part in formal organizations such as the *Foster Grandparent Programs* or in their neighborhood where, for whatever reason, they may "adopt" a child. We also classified foster parents as well as grandparents who adopt their grandchildren as surrogates. One of the most important observations made of this group was their willingness to reach far beyond their own families to help children in difficult situations such as family disruption, abuse, physical and mental challenges, and trouble with the law. Surrogate grandparenting is on the rise—a group needing encouragement and support from the community as they attempt to bridge a gap many would never consider.

Kay Smith, a social worker and lawyer, contributed a chapter on grandparenting and the law. She provides an overview of the legal dimensions of grandparenting. Kay's chapter identifies and briefly discusses a variety of grandparenting issues. Likewise, she speaks of the importance of having a legal counselor who is aware of the issues as well as strategies for resolving problems that are an outgrowth of our legal system.

One chapter that might possibly be a surprise is on great-grandparenting. The surprise is the probability that the majority of grandparents in the future will live long enough to be great-grandparents. This relatively invisible career was described as one in uncharted territory.

After reading this book, please consider this question: As a grandparent or a great-grandparent, how are you doing in this career dedicated to the grandchildren that mean so much to you? There are many possible answers to this question. Some might respond by saying, "I'm just the way I want to be. Thank you." If that is your answer, please consider helping other grandparents that may not be as sure of their career as you. You may even want to write an article.

You may find yourself in more than one of the categories discussed. Which, if any, should take priority in your grandparenting career? You might want to look at your values, your resources, and the family situation, and then prioritize which one should be given the top position. You might divide your time among the various types. If you spend time with other grandparents in each of these categories, you might gain valuable insights that will help in your own situations.

Perhaps you have been a religious person most of your life, but you have not always integrated your spiritual life with the life lived before your grandchildren. You might ask the question: "Is it too late for me to leave a spiritual legacy?" Hopefully, after reflecting on your question you will decide that it is never too late. Spend time reading and making application of the scriptures. Make prayer a part of your daily life. You can pray at any time, any place. Every time you think of your grandchildren, pause, give God thanks for those children, and ask for guidance as you fulfill your grandparenting career.

Marc Freidman calls the grandparenting time of life "prime time." He advocates that the "aging opportunity" before us has not been realized. He gives several reasons for this situation, which can be summarized by saying, "There is a cultural lag in every part of our society that prevents us from realizing our potential through our whole life." This cultural lag is especially true of the grandparenting career. The "aging opportunity" Friedman discusses in his book needs to be integrated into the lives of all grandparents, especially in light of the longevity revolution. As grandparents, don't become a captive of your culture. Recognize the newness of this career and the many paths it can take.[41] As Emerson so well stated, "Do not go where the path may lead, go instead where there is no path and leave a trail." May you and your grandparenting career have the successes, joys, and blessings that are inherent in grandparenting and "God shall supply all your needs according to his riches in glory" Phillipians 4:9, TLV.

If, in the future, we can be of further service to you or your organization, please feel free to contact us at www.derrelrw@highervaluesolutions.com, or dickersonbe@yahoo.com.

---

41   Marc Freedman, *Prime Time: How Baby Boomers Will Revolutionize Retirement and Transform America.*(New York: BBS-Public Affairs, 1999).

Prayer

Dear Lord, may the reading of this book encourage us to be all that you desire in loving and caring for our grandchildren. Help us to rely on the Bible for direction, encouragement, and comfort. You have blessed us with this amazing experience to be grandparents. Even as we pray for ourselves, we pray for our grandchildren that they may see Jesus in the way we live and speak. We are committed to praying daily for these children so they may have the confidence and joy that is possible only through a relationship with you. Thank you for the blessing of being grandparents. Amen.

Endnotes

1   Charles S, Swindoll, in *Seniors' Devotional Bible, New International Version,* (Grand Rapids: Zondervan), 714.

2   Both of the primary authors of this book can testify that Lance's grandparents did an exceptional job in rearing him to be a fine man and a wonderful Christian gentleman. We asked him to write this chapter because of our appreciation of him and his accomplishments.

NOTES

NOTES

NOTES

NOTES